Praise for *Wired to Care*

"*Wired to Care* describes how to recover the basic human abilities of empathy that may be buried by your day-to-day business routines. Dev Patnaik shows how you can create a more empathic—and much more successful—business."

—**Chip Heath**, author of *Made to Stick*

"*Wired to Care* will convince you that businesses succeed with their hearts as much as their heads. Dev Patnaik has given us just what we need for the lean years ahead."

—**Malcolm Gladwell**, author of *Outliers*, *Blink*, and *The Tipping Point*

"Dev Patnaik's *Wired to Care* maps a path to innovation fueled by 'seeing the world with new eyes.' On numerous occasions, Dev and his colleagues at Jump helped us break through to those most critical insights."

—**Beth Comstock**, Chief Marketing Officer, GE

"Empathy might be the most underappreciated ability in business. But with this smart and insightful book, Dev Patnaik shows how to enlist this powerful capacity both to boost your own business and to better our shared world."

—**Daniel H. Pink**, author of *A Whole New Mind*

"*Wired to Care* offers a roadmap to success paved with empathy, where caring contributes more to the potential success of a company than cost cutting, and where hope is more important than hype. The bottom line is better profits, better products, and happier employees. There is a better day for business (thankfully) when companies are wired to care."

—**Robyn Waters**, former VP of Trend, Target Stores and author of *The Hummer and the Mini*

WIRED *to* CARE

WIRED *to* CARE

*how companies prosper when they
create widespread empathy*

DEV PATNAIK
with Peter Mortensen

Vice President, Publisher: Tim Moore
Associate Publisher and Director of Marketing: Amy Neidlinger
Acquisitions Editor: Martha Cooley
Editorial Assistant: Heather Luciano
Operations Manager: Gina Kanouse
Digital Marketing Manager: Julie Phifer
Publicity Manager: Laura Czaja
Assistant Marketing Manager: Megan Colvin
Marketing Assistant: Brandon Smith
Cover Designer: Ann Liu
Managing Editor: Kristy Hart
Senior Project Editor: Lori Lyons
Copy Editor: Krista Hansing Editorial Services, Inc.
Proofreader: San Dee Philips
Senior Indexer: Cheryl Lenser
Interior Designer/Composition: Bumpy Design
Manufacturing Buyer: Dan Uhrig

Published by FT Press
Upper Saddle River, New Jersey 07458

FT Press offers excellent discounts on this book when ordered in quantity for bulk purchases
or special sales. For more information, please contact U.S. Corporate and Government Sales,
1-800-382-3419, corpsales@pearsontechgroup.com. For sales outside the U.S., please contact
International Sales at international@pearson.com.

Third Printing May 2009

ISBN-10: 0-13-714234-X
ISBN-13: 978-0-13-714234-7

Pearson Education LTD.
Pearson Education Australia PTY, Limited
Pearson Education Singapore, Pte. Ltd.
Pearson Education North Asia, Ltd.
Pearson Education Canada, Ltd.
Pearson Educación de Mexico, S.A. de C.V.
Pearson Education—Japan
Pearson Education Malaysia, Pte. Ltd.

Library of Congress Cataloging-in-Publication Data

Patnaik, Dev, 1970-
 Wired to care : how companies prosper when they create widespread empathy / Dev Patnaik
with Peter Mortensen.
    p. cm.
 ISBN 0-13-714234-X (hardback : alk. paper) 1. Organizational effectiveness. 2. Empathy. 3.
Interpersonal relations. 4. Success in business--Psychological aspects. I. Mortensen, Peter,
1981- II. Title.
  HD58.9.P38 2009
  658.8'343--dc22
                          2008024346

For My Parents,
Who made me all that I am.

Contents

PART I   The Case for Empathy

ONE

Introduction 3

Companies prosper when they tap into a power that every one of us already has—the ability to reach outside of ourselves and connect with other people.

TWO

The Map Is Not the Territory 19

Empathy is an antidote to a world of abstraction. Faced with a deluge of information, people like to boil things down. This puts them in danger of making poor decisions based on incomplete or distorted information.

THREE

The Way Things Used to Be 42

Empathy isn't a new phenomenon. There was a time not so long ago when there was a broad and deep connection between producers and consumers that allowed everyone to prosper.

PART II   Creating Widespread Empathy

FOUR

The Power of Affinity 67

The quickest way to have empathy for someone else is to be just like them. For companies, the answer is to hire their customers.

FIVE

Walking in Someone Else's Shoes 85

It's often not possible or not enough to hire your customers. To continue to grow and prosper, you have to step outside of yourself and walk in someone else's shoes.

SIX

Empathy That Lasts 105

Bringing people face to face triggers a caring response. The emotionally charged memories of that experience can be a guiding light to stay true to the vision.

SEVEN

Open All the Windows 124

While having empathy for other people is a good thing for us to do as individuals, it's far more powerful when you can create widespread empathy throughout a large organization.

PART III   The Results of Empathy

EIGHT

Reframe How You See the World 143

When you step outside of yourself, you open up to the possibility of seeing new opportunities for growth.

NINE

We Are Them and They Are Us 165

When companies create an empathic connection to the rest of the world, a funny thing starts to happen. The line between outside and in, between producer and consumer, begins to blur.

TEN

The Golden Rule 180

Consistent ethical behavior demands that you walk in other people's shoes. Because of this, Widespread Empathy can be an effective way to ensure the morality of a large institution, more so than any rulebook or code of conduct.

ELEVEN

The Hidden Payoff 200

Having empathy for others can do more than drive growth. It can also give people the one thing that too many of us lack: a reason to come in to work every day.

Acknowledgments 217
Endnotes 223
Index 237
About the Authors 251

PART I

The Case for Empathy

ONE

Introduction

*Companies prosper when they tap into a power that
every one of us already has—the ability to reach
outside of ourselves and connect with other people.*

EARLY ONE MORNING in 1979, Pattie Moore did a peculiar thing. A young designer living in New York, she woke up, got out of bed, and started to make herself frail. She strapped herself into a body brace that made her shoulders hunch forward. She hid her auburn locks under a white wig and painted her eyelashes gray. She plugged up her ears so she couldn't hear. And she put on horn-rimmed glasses that blurred her vision. Transformed into a woman more than three times her actual age, Pattie headed out into the world, a wooden cane guiding her path. Leaving her Gramercy Park walk-up, Pattie stepped out into a land that was unlike any she had ever experienced. Pattie had made herself old, and now even her own neighborhood looked strange to her.

Weeks earlier, Pattie had been involved in a planning discussion for the design of a new refrigerator. She had just landed a job at the offices of Raymond Loewy, an icon of twentieth century industrial design. Sitting in a brainstorming session, Pattie listened as the other designers traded ideas for what the new fridge might look like. After a little while, she raised her hand.

Perhaps the team should consider how to accommodate the needs of people with arthritis, poor vision, or reduced strength. Pattie had grown up with her grandparents at home. She vividly remembered how her grandmother had been forced to stop cooking when the infirmities of old age made it impossible to peel a potato, open a carton of milk, or even pull a refrigerator door open. Now, given the chance to design a new fridge, she wondered if there wasn't a way to help other people's grandmothers to continue to cook as they got older. The other designers stared at her blankly. "Pattie," one shrugged, "we don't design for those people."

That moment changed the course of Pattie's career. It seemed obvious to her that there were a lot of people in the world who were like her grandmother. And yet, there were clearly more than a few designers who weren't interested in designing for anyone besides themselves. So she decided to change things. At the same time, Pattie realized that she herself had little real empathy for senior citizens, if only because she had never experienced the world as they did. And that's when she started to plan her experiment.

Pattie decided to simulate what it was like to be old so that she might figure out what life was like for her elders. With the help of a friend who worked as a television make-up artist, she transformed herself into an eighty-five-year-old woman. As she quickly found out, when you're old, the world isn't designed for you. Pill bottles demanded too much dexterity. Telephones were too hard to dial. Climbing the steps onto a city bus was a dangerous ordeal. Occasionally, strangers would stop to lend a hand with momentary tasks, but the second they walked away, she was once again left to make it on her own in a world where the deck was stacked against her. To make matters worse, people ignored her or made jokes at her expense. It was if she wasn't a person anymore. Pattie saw, heard, and, more than anything else, felt all of this pain as she went about her business. The experience was agonizing. Everywhere she looked, Pattie saw opportunities to make things better. Everything needed to be fixed.

Pattie continued her experiment for the next three years, going undercover in more than a hundred cities throughout the United States and Canada. Every time, her routine was the same. Wake up, become old, and see the world through new eyes. And over the course of her journeys, Pattie came to see things differently. Getting old wasn't really the problem. It was everything else. If your hand couldn't get a potato peeler to work, maybe there was something wrong with the peeler. If you weren't strong enough to pull a door open, maybe the problem was the door. Perhaps so-called disabilities were caused by products and architecture, not by age and health.

Pattie's experience would end up pointing the way for an entirely new generation of designers, ones more attuned to the world around them. It also revealed huge business opportunities that had been overlooked for years. Based on her work, companies as diverse as Boeing, Merck, and Toyota developed new offerings that grew their businesses and differentiated their products. It turns out that senior citizens aren't just some niche market—they reflect unarticulated needs that many of us have. When you make doors that are easier for seniors to open, you make life easier for all of us, young and old.

Through her work, Pattie Moore has helped to make life a little bit more livable for people in many parts of the world. In doing so, she also revealed an important but oft-forgotten truism: People discover unseen opportunities when they have a personal and empathic connection with the world around them. For individuals, that means developing the ability to walk in other people's shoes. For companies and other large institutions, that means finding a way to bring the rest of the world inside their walls.

EMPATHY EQUALS GROWTH

This is the story of how companies, and indeed organizations of all kinds, prosper when they tap into a power that every one of us already has: the ability to reach outside ourselves and connect with other people. And it's the story of how institutions can so easily lose their way when their people lose that connection. Human beings are intrinsically social animals. Our brains have developed subtle and sophisticated ways to understand what other people are thinking and feeling. Simply put, we're wired to care. We rely on those instincts to help us make better decisions in situations that affect the folks around us. Unfortunately, that instinct seems to get short-circuited when we get together in large groups. We lose our intuition, our gut sense for what's going on outside of that group. Corporations become more insular. Colleges start to feel like ivory towers. Political campaigns take on a "bunker mentality." That sort of isolation can have disastrous effects because these same institutions depend on the outside world for revenues and reputation and votes.

When people in an organization develop a shared and intuitive vibe for what's going on in the world, they're able to see new opportunities faster than their competitors, long before that information becomes explicit enough to read about in *The Wall Street Journal*. They have the courage of their convictions to take a risk on something new. And they have the gut-level intuition to see how their actions impact the people who matter most: the folks who buy their products, interact with their brand, and ultimately fund their 401(k) plans. That intuition transcends what's traditionally referred to as market research. A widespread sense of empathy starts to influence the culture of a place, giving it a sense of clarity and mission. People spend less time arguing about things that ultimately don't matter. Empathy can even start to ensure more ethical behavior in a way that no policies and procedures manual ever could.

Wired to Care is nominally a business book. But it seeks to answer questions that are relevant to businesspeople, educators, designers, marketers, athletes, policymakers, and citizens alike. How can we nurture the instinct that all human beings have to walk in other people's shoes? How can we, in turn, create a wider sense of empathy to connect larger organizations to the world around them? And how can we leverage that widespread empathy to be an engine for growth and change?

In pursuit of the answers, we'll explore how large institutions lose their connection with the outside world, how they can regain their sense of empathy, and what the results look like when they do. We'll visit Zildjian, one of the oldest companies in the world, and see how they've prospered for nearly 400 years by connecting with superstar clientele, from Turkish emperors to Philadelphia hip-hop groups. We'll dive deep into the catacombs of the human brain, to find the biological sources of empathy, and discover how mirror neurons and the limbic system enable us to feel what others are feeling. And we'll spend time on both sides of the political aisle, with James Carville, the Ragin' Cajun, and John McCain, a national hero, to show how first-hand life experience can give you the acuity to cut through a morass of otherwise confusing and contradictory information. We'll spend time at big companies like IBM, Target, and Intel. But we'll also go to farmers' markets and a conference on world religions. All of this is to reclaim a very old idea, that quantitative data and facts are no substitute for real-world experience and human connection.

This book is divided into three sections. The first seeks to make the case for why empathy matters: how organizations lose sight of the real world and how they might regain that connection. The second section explores the mechanisms that allow human beings to connect with others and how we can create a widespread sense of empathy across a large group of people. The last section describes the payoff. It shows how widespread empathy can help companies to see opportunities faster, prosper for longer, ensure ethical conduct, and instill a personal sense of meaning in each of us as individuals.

As one of the founders of Jump Associates, I work with companies to help them find new opportunities for growth. I have the privilege of working with the leaders of some of the world's most innovative companies, foundations, and public institutions. Some of them are people you see profiled in newspapers and magazines. Others are folks you've never heard of but probably should have. I also spend time teaching designers and business school students at Stanford University. In the course of my work, I've received a lot of requests to talk to groups about innovation. And I tell them that the problem with business today isn't a lack of innovation; it's a lack of empathy. As you can imagine, that statement can cause some very different reactions, depending on whether I'm talking to toy designers or oil industry executives. It's amazing how quickly business people write off something that sounds too soft. But empathy is more than a warm and fuzzy notion best-suited for annual reports and greeting cards. It's the ability to step outside of yourself and see the world as other people do. For many of the world's greatest companies, it's an ever-present but rarely talked-about engine for growth.

REFLECT WHAT YOU SEE

The simplest way to have empathy for other people is to be just like them. Studies show that girls have an easier time understanding other girls and boys find it easier to understand other boys. People with common political leanings demonstrate a similar ability to connect. For companies, it's not surprising, then, that the quickest way to gain empathy is to hire your customers. Harley-Davidson is a great example of a company that has generated a widespread sense of empathy based on their employees' own experiences as riders. And that empathy starts in the parking lot.

A parking lot says a lot about a company. It can reflect an organization's hierarchy, its values, and how it sees the world. Some companies reserve the first row of parking for their customers. Others designate the best spots for senior management. At Harley-Davidson's headquarters, in Milwaukee, Wisconsin, a posted metal sign clearly states the company's priorities: "No cages. Motorcycle parking only." The second sentence is a translation for guests who don't speak motorcycle slang. Cages are what riders call automobiles, vehicles that lock people away from the wide, open world. You just drove over in a Ford Taurus that you rented at the airport? Welcome to Harley-Davidson. Parking is in the back.

Visitors to the company's headquarters soon discover that the parking lot rule is a sign of things to come. Harley-Davidson's office is a shrine to the motorcycle culture that the company has helped to create. Walking down an aisle of otherwise ordinary office cubicles, you're confronted by an endless display of photos, signs, and exquisitely painted motorcycle gas tanks. On one wall, snapshots capture scenes from one employee's recent bike ride down the Gulf Coast of Florida. Other walls proudly display banners from rallies and other events, including the pilgrimage that hundreds of thousands of riders make every year to Sturgis, South Dakota. Each floor of the building is named for a different Harley engine, from the V-Twin to the Evolution. Tables in the conference rooms are constructed from sheets of glass balanced on top of engine blocks. In some parts of the building, the air itself smells like leather.

Interesting and eclectic, the motorcycle memorabilia at Harley-Davidson isn't just for show. Every picture is a trophy, a placeholder for the larger story that Harley-Davidson's riders write together, customers and employees alike. People walking through the office invariably sport T-shirts and vests emblazoned with logos and place names, their clothing helping to paint a picture of the Harley lifestyle.

What's striking about Harley-Davidson is how people throughout the company, from the engineers in manufacturing to the accountants in finance, have an intuitive understanding of the riders who buy their products. The company cherishes this relationship and goes so far as to mandate that leaders throughout the organization spend measurable amounts of time out with motorcycle riders. It's important to point out that riding a motorcycle isn't a prerequisite to work at Harley-Davidson. Many people at the company don't. Nevertheless, the company is able to instill its values in employees who've never ridden a bike. It's not enough for Harley to simply hire its customers. Riders must have empathy with nonriders and vice versa. Cages are as unwelcome in Harley-Davidson's business philosophy as they are in its parking lot.

Harley's greatest period of success so far occurred between 1986 and 2006. While American car companies lost billions of dollars and laid off employees in ever-greater numbers, Harley enjoyed uninterrupted double-digit growth. Conventional wisdom dictated that U.S. companies entrenched in manufacturing were burdened with high labor costs and excessive benefits packages, but Harley continued to make its motorcycles where it always has, in Wisconsin, while paying top dollar to its unionized workforce. Harley motorcycles commanded a premium over competitors from Japan and Europe, and people snapped up every single unit that the company could produce. A Harley-Davidson motorcycle came to stand in a class by itself, revered for the distinctive growl of its engine and the out-of-bounds lifestyle it evoked. The timeframe of Harley's sustained boom is no coincidence; that's when Harley made widespread empathy a key element of corporate strategy.

Before that, the company was on the verge of bankruptcy as strong Japanese competitors eroded market share and introduced cheaper, lighter models that undercut all of Harley's product line. In response, Harley refocused its attention away from itself and onto the people who rode its motorcycles. They energized the Harley Owners Group into an army of evangelists. Harley transformed itself into an icon of American freedom. The widespread empathy that Harley employees had for riders helped them make a thousand better decisions every day. Harley-Davidson commercialized new opportunities faster than its competitors, entered new businesses before success was certain, and enjoyed customer loyalty that was the envy of every other organization in the world.

When organizations like Harley are able to create that widespread sense of empathy, something interesting starts to happen. Over time, that implicit connection to the outside world helps blur the line between producers and consumers. Between inside the building and out. Between us and them. Harley likes to call the folks who buy its motorcycles riders, not customers, if only because so many Harley employees are riders themselves. As Lara Lee, Harley-Davidson's former head of services so aptly put it, "We don't spend a lot of time talking about 'what consumers want.' So far as we're concerned, we are them and they are us."

Harley's connection to riders is so strong that it raises an interesting long-term challenge for the company, whose decades of earnings growth began to slow in 2007. How will Harley-Davidson connect to a new generation of young people who don't want to ride what their parents did?

STEPPING OUTSIDE OF YOURSELF

Harley's imminent challenge is one that many organizations share. It isn't always possible to be your customers (consider, for instance, a pharmaceutical company that makes drugs for terminally ill patients). In those cases, it's necessary to do something more than reflect what you see. To continue to grow and prosper, you have to get outside of yourself and see the world through the eyes of other people.

Gina Beebe does that as much as anyone. She's the head of design at American Girl, a doll maker and book publisher that's beloved by young girls and parents alike. American Girl was founded by Pleasant Rowland, a uniquely imaginative leader who dedicated her life to creating dolls and stories that would help girls learn and grow. Each doll represents a different time and place in America, from Kaya, a Nez Perce Native American from 1764, to Julie, a girl with divorced parents living in 1974 San Francisco. American Girl does more than just make dolls—they make compelling stories that resonate deeply with how girls see the world. That's hard to do year after year. I asked Gina how she does that, given that she herself isn't an eight-year-old girl. She thought about it for a moment and then smiled, "You know...in a way, I kind of am." Gina talked about the joy she gets from seeing little girls flock to the company's newest dolls and books.

And how she spends time reading the letters that young girls write to the company. And how the company posts those letters in the hallways for everyone to read and enjoy. Gina and the folks at American Girl are a wonderful example of how you can get yourself into someone else's mindset—and how that person's feelings can, in turn, get into you.

The ability to reach outside of yourself is even more important when you consider situations in which you need empathy for more than one type of person. Doctors, for example, can't have empathy for only other patients their own age. Teachers can't connect only with students who share their gender or ethnicity. For companies who seek to serve many different types of people, merely reflecting a single point of view isn't enough. Indeed, the ability to empathize with *multiple* types of people can be the difference between success and failure over the long term.

The ability of Gina Beebe and her colleagues to step into the mind of an eight-year-old is the real secret behind American Girl's success. It requires them to leave their own agendas behind, and actually care about how other people see the world. That's a powerful concept, but not a particularly new one. In fact, it was Dale Carnegie who first articulated that dynamic nearly a century ago, in his book *How to Win Friends and Influence People*. Carnegie was one of the world's first modern self-help gurus, and when you're the first, you don't need to be particularly surprising or counter-intuitive. In fact, his point was deceptively simple: If you want people to be interested in you, you should be genuinely interested in other people. That's a pretty straightforward lesson with relatively major implications. It means that if you walk up to me at a party and ask me how I am, how my family is doing, what movies I've seen lately, and how things are going at work, you're bound to get me engaged. In fact, by the time you walk away, I'll be thinking, "Wow, I just met a really interesting person." That's because we talked about something I'm interested in—me! It's just human nature to be interested in people who are interested in you. That little bit of advice can go a long way to making a person more likeable. It's also a profound piece of advice for business. If you want to create products and services that other people care about, you should put aside your problems and start caring about other people's lives.

Creating that sort of empathic connection to other people can have profound effects on a company, beyond increasing its growth rate. In many cases, it can give new meaning to the work that people do. And often in today's world, it's that sense of meaning that we lack most of all. Most companies can offer competitive salaries, vacation packages, health insurance, and retirement plans. But too few of them can demonstrate any sort of connection between the work that we do everyday and a positive impact on the wider world. Beyond mere survival and provision for our families, many of us don't have a good reason to go to work in the morning. In addition to its economic impacts, increasing empathy for the people your company serves can help you see how much your job makes a difference in their lives. And that's the greatest reward of all.

FROM XBOX TO ZUNE

We began this introduction with an example of how empathy can help individuals to see the world in a completely different way. We end with an example from one of the largest companies on the planet, and how empathy helped it succeed in a radically new venture.

By the spring of 1999, the game console business had become far too big for Microsoft to ignore. Company executives had watched as pioneers like Atari, and then Nintendo, developed the fledgling industry, built a fan base, and made it financially viable for both console manufacturers and game developers alike. But then, in the mid-1990s, Sony took the business to a whole new level. Sony had leveraged its vast technical capabilities to make PlayStation a worldwide success. Now, Sony was readying the launch of PlayStation 2. The PS2 was much more than the toys that had come before it. The console was a high-powered entertainment engine capable of playing DVD movies, importing digital video, and connecting to the Internet. And it did it all without using a single line of Microsoft programming code. Having successfully fought off rivals like IBM, Apple, and Netscape, Microsoft now faced the prospect of irrelevance as younger people came to spend more time on their video game consoles and less time on their PCs. Microsoft had little choice but to act.

The company was starting at a distinct disadvantage. Sony was the most powerful consumer electronics maker on the planet. It had years of experience to build on and a vast library of games that were hugely popular. Microsoft, by comparison, had relatively little experience in designing and selling hardware. The company wouldn't be able to put out its console until late 2001, by which time PS2 would likely be in 10 million households. More troublingly, Microsoft's experience in operating systems and office applications left it with very little feel for the new business.

To win, Microsoft was prepared to spend billions of dollars from its vast cash reserves without the promise of seeing a profit for many years to come. Recognizing that it was entering unfamiliar territory, the company set about assembling a team of engineers, designers, and marketers and charged them with creating the ultimate game console.

The developers decided that they shouldn't try to be everything to everyone. And they weren't going to focus on kids. Unlike Nintendo and Sony, Microsoft wouldn't build a console that would let prepubescent moppets play with magic mushrooms and fairy princesses who needed to be rescued. The team envisioned a game system that would serve up playable versions of action movies, with testosterone-fueled experiences that were even more immersive than any summer blockbuster. The new machine would be for hardcore gamers—the kind of guys who loved to kick some ass. Guys who spent hours playing intense, complicated, and sometimes violent computer games that got their blood rushing. Guys like...themselves.

Two years later, Microsoft launched the Xbox, which used the same electronics as a high-end PC, including a built-in hard drive. Its case was huge, knobby, and eye-scorchingly green and black. Xbox's signature game was *Halo*, an intense first-person shooter game that starred a masked hero known as the Master Chief who traveled across galaxies to repel hostile aliens.

Xbox was an overnight sensation in the United States. More than 5 million copies of *Halo* were sold, making it the top-selling title of its generation. More important, *Halo* helped define the Xbox as the must-have console for hardcore gamers. Although Sony was still able to outpace Microsoft on the strength of PS2, Microsoft used Xbox to shift the momentum. Xbox's next version, the Xbox 360, outpaced Sony's new PlayStation 3 in the United States by a margin of two to one. Microsoft had successfully found a way to compete with Sony. Less than a decade after entering the market, Xbox accounted for ten percent of Microsoft's total revenue and an even greater percentage of its top-line growth.

Xbox was so successful that Microsoft turned to the same scrappy team of developers when Apple's iPod became the best-selling portable music player since the Sony Walkman. If the Xbox guys had done so well against Sony, surely they could do the same thing to Apple. On an incredibly tight deadline, the team that worked magic on Xbox threw its collective might behind an iPod-killer. What emerged in Fall 2006, however, barely dented Apple's armor. The Zune was a boxy gadget that looked like a thicker iPod, albeit in a not-so-stylish brown case. The interface was cumbersome and seemed designed for no one in particular. As one acid-tongued reviewer described it, the overall experience of using a Zune was about as pleasant as having an airbag deploy in your face. Not surprisingly, the Zune managed to sell about 2 million units in its first 18 months on the market. Apple sold more than 84 million iPods during that same period. Apple's dominance in the music player market remained untouched.

Why was the Microsoft team able to create such a compelling video game system only to churn out a mediocre portable music player? What makes a team deliver bravura performances one day and a fiasco the next? Here again, empathy played a huge part. As one member of the team confided, "The biggest challenge with Zune was trying to figure out who we were building it for. With Xbox, we knew those guys. Hell, we *were* those guys."

Microsoft succeeded with Xbox because it was able to leverage the empathy of its development team. Unfortunately, that empathy wasn't transferable. A brilliant connection with hardcore gamers didn't prepare Microsoft for the challenges of understanding Zune's market space. Being a reflection of one type of customer is certainly a quick and easy way to connect with a particular group of people. But to thrive over the long term, organizations need to move beyond their own views and discover what's happening in the rest of the world. They need to step outside themselves to see the world through other people's eyes. People are wired to care. Organizations need to be wired to care, as well. When that happens, the effects of empathy can be profound. Companies prosper. Communities thrive. And we all have a better day at work.

TWO

The Map Is Not the Territory

*Empathy is an antidote to a world of abstraction.
Faced with a deluge of information, people
like to boil things down. This puts them in
danger of making poor decisions based on
incomplete or distorted information.*

BY 1908, MOST TRAVELERS on the London Underground could agree on one thing: It was easy to get lost on the Tube. This was not surprising, since the system was really a bolted-together hodgepodge of what had been no less than ten different rail lines. In an effort to clarify matters, the operators of the Underground decided to publish a map to show how all its lines were interconnected. With great fanfare, they launched their new map through a citywide promotional campaign. Yet despite their best efforts, the map was a failure.

Because London isn't laid out along a regular grid, the lines of the Tube follow circuitous, looping paths across the city. Although the map was an accurate depiction of these twists and turns, it ended up looking like Technicolor spaghetti. The addition of aboveground landmarks only made the map harder to read. If you had never visited London before and wanted to get from Westminster Station to Paddington Station, consulting the map was little help. The map of the London Underground was accurate, comprehensive, and nearly useless.

Confusion reigned until a laid-off employee of the Underground, 29-year-old Harry Beck, saw a way out of the mapping problem. He realized that people who used a map of the Underground didn't need to know each bend in the track or even the precise distance between stops; they just needed to know how to get from one station to the next. Tube travelers didn't need a map of London. They needed a diagram of the Underground.

In a small notebook, Beck sketched out an almost preposterously simplified image of the entire Underground system. He drew every rail line in London as either a horizontal, vertical, or 45-degree diagonal line. He eliminated every geographic landmark except for the Thames River, which he reduced to a set of geometric segments. He drew the distance between each stop as the same length, whether the actual distance was 200 yards or two miles. And he increased the size of the city's center to make it easier to read the names of the many stations contained in London's densest districts. In a few minutes of sketching, he reduced the most complex transit system on earth into something a child could understand.

Today, Beck's famous diagram is one of the most beloved maps in the world. Numerous other cities, from Moscow to Tokyo, have used its design as inspiration for their own transit maps. That said, the London Underground Map is not without its problems. In the interest of simplicity, the map isn't to scale, which creates a false impression of the London that exists aboveground. Twists in the rail line and distances between two points become exaggerated or compressed on Beck's map based on how far you are from the center. As a result, riding the Tube between two points that appear close together can end up taking more than an hour, while walking between those same locations might take just fifteen minutes. Conversely, walking between two adjacent stations located far from London's center can feel like a daytrip.

Beck's map gives you only one type of information: which Tube lines you need to take if, for example, you want to go from Paddington to Covent Garden. It won't, however, tell you how to find the out-of-the-way curry joint that you're looking for in Covent Garden, whether the restaurant is any good, or whether the train is the best way to get there. That's because Beck's map was designed for precisely one purpose: helping travelers to get from one London station to another by underground rail. That's it. As a guide to the London Underground, Beck's map is a work of genius. But it's no substitute for actually visiting London. The map is not the territory.

Alfred Korzybski, a Polish-American philosopher, first articulated that idea in a paper he presented to the American Mathematical Society in 1931. Korzybski observed that people are great at pattern identification. We have the innate ability to take in a myriad of data through our senses and then boil it all down into easily digestible models. But sometimes we forget that our models are merely a representation of reality, not reality itself. Reading about what life is like for the elderly isn't the same as being old yourself. Analyzing digital music preferences isn't enough to help you design an MP3 player that people will love. Any effort to capture reality so it can be shared with another person necessarily leaves out a lot of contextual information.

The importance of Korzybski's point becomes clear when we consider how businesses have come to deal with information. Over the last hundred years, we've created increasingly sophisticated systems for trying to figure out what's really going on inside and outside of a company. That's generally a good thing. It used to be that one part of a large organization never had any idea what was going on in another. Factories would run out of bolts before anyone realized that they needed to order more. Stores would all get the same amount of goods, even though sales of a product were taking off in one part of the country and moving slowly in another. Because there was no good way to share information, business decision making relied on a lot of conventional wisdom and unsubstantiated hearsay.

All of that changed as businesses started to aggregate and analyze information in real time. Operations experts have created analytical systems that can perform incredible calculations on a given set of data, such as inventory or supply chain. Today, when you buy a sweater at a mall near your house, your purchase triggers a message that affects how much pigment is getting ordered to dye a batch of wool in Spain. Most managers can pull up a snapshot of important indicators of their business at a moment's notice, including growth, market trends, and productivity. They use these tools to get a coherent picture of what's happening throughout the entire company. This has created a fact-based approach to decision making that has taken a lot of the voodoo out of business.

The information revolution has also led to the creation of a lot of "maps," including strategic plans, sales forecasts, and manufacturing quality reports. Like Beck's Underground map, these reports are abstractions. Yet companies have become so dependent on these models that many organizations have started to lose touch with reality. Like the London visitor who takes the Underground to a destination that could be reached more quickly by walking, many companies end up following courses of action that are sensible within their models but unsuited to the real world.

This fact-based approach also extends to how companies deal with external data—information about the people who buy their products and services. Firms have created maps—market segmentations, research reports, even video compilations—to help aggregate information about the activities, motivations, and needs of everyday people. Those maps are a poor substitute for actual human contact. Lacking firsthand experience, far too many managers are making critical decisions without any personal feel for the territory.

More than one business leader has complained to me that their company is attracting smart and ambitious young people who lack any sort of gut sense for the work they do. In our search for compelling data about business, we may have created an entire generation of assistant marketing managers who believe that they understand their business if they have five good bullets on a PowerPoint page. They forget that PowerPoint is an abstraction and that their marketing plan is only a map. They don't know the territory.

Business happens out in the real world: in stores, on streets, and in homes. And anyone can develop empathy by spending more time in those places. Empathy can provide the necessary context for decision makers to see the implications of their actions. It can make otherwise abstract data seem real and immediate. And it can help develop the experience required to judge the accuracy of any map. Without personal connection to the people they serve, companies lack the context, immediacy, or experience they need to make good decisions. As a result, far too many leaders make critical decisions without any personal feel for the territory. Without that empathy, organizations can start to lose their way a little bit at a time. The rise and fall of the American coffee industry is a well-documented example of such a scenario.

MAXWELL HOUSE DESTROYS COFFEE

People assume that great-tasting coffee is a recent phenomenon in the United States. Nothing could be further from the truth.

In the 1950s, you could get a great-tasting cup of joe anywhere in the country for a nickel. America was a nation hooked on coffee. But just at the moment when demand for coffee was booming, its supply fell into disarray. In late June 1953, a killer frost wiped out almost the entire Brazilian coffee crop, sending wholesale prices soaring. After what came to be known as The Fourth of July Frost, the price of a cup of coffee shot up to a dime and even higher as American coffee roasters like Maxwell House, Folgers, and Hills Bros. scrambled to keep up with demand.

It's never a good idea to get in between a committed coffee drinker and his daily cup. The higher prices infuriated Americans. Consumers staged protests in diners and wrote angry letters to coffee company executives. Politicians and newspapers accused Latin American governments of artificially limiting exports to exploit the U.S. market. The supply problems that American coffee companies faced had turned into a public relations disaster. Coffee companies became convinced that they needed to cut their expenses drastically or face the very real possibility that the American love affair with coffee was about to come to an end. In desperation, they did the unthinkable: They played the Robusta card.

Of the many subvarieties of coffee beans, two major categories predominate, Arabica and Robusta. Arabica is a gently bitter, temptingly smooth, and nutty variety that carries within it all the flavors we look forward to when we order a cup of coffee. But as American coffee companies had discovered, Arabica trees are also expensive to raise and highly vulnerable to bad weather and parasites. One year might yield a bumper crop. The next could be a bust. After the frost of 1953, it became clear that Arabica was far too fragile a plant for coffee companies to base their long-term futures on. They needed to find a more reliable coffee bean. Enter Robusta beans, which are cheap, impervious to the elements, and plentiful. They also produce coffee that's nearly undrinkable. For decades, major American coffee makers had resisted using Robusta beans in any of their products. Now faced with dwindling Arabica supplies, managers at Maxwell House started to reconsider that decision. Perhaps, they speculated, it would be possible to add just a few Robusta beans to Maxwell House's blend without noticeably ruining the taste. If successful, the overall blend would be much cheaper than pure Arabica.

The Robusta content would have to be negligible—it was important that no one notice the unwelcome addition. To ensure that Maxwell House wouldn't lose any customers through this cost-cutting measure, the company ran sensory tests in which people tasted coffee made with Robusta right alongside the traditional Maxwell House blend. Almost no one could tell the difference. The company decided to launch the new blend. By supplementing its blend with Robusta, Maxwell House was able to keep costs lower while its competitors were forced to raise prices. The company's gamble on Robusta paid off immediately. Most consumers didn't notice any difference, and Robusta helped keep coffee prices low. Other coffee companies quickly followed suit. No one complained.

While Maxwell House had found a way to protect profits for the short term, it hadn't been able to solve the coffee industry's long-term problem. Demand for coffee would continue to grow, and Arabica beans remained scarce. The following year, continued pressures on margins forced Maxwell House managers to again consider modifying the blend. Consumers hadn't noticed the addition of a small amount of Robusta beans the first time around. Would they be able to tell if Maxwell House added a little bit more? There was only one way to know. The company ordered another round of consumer tests. Thankfully, these, too,

came back with positive results. Consumers couldn't tell the difference between the slightly increased levels of Robusta and the
previous blend.

And so it went for several years. Demand for coffee continued to rise. The pressure on profits was equally unrelenting. And
each year, Maxwell House, together with Folgers and Hills Bros.,
increased the percentage of Robusta beans in their coffee blends
by a nearly imperceptible amount. Every year, coffee makers
turned to consumer testing to ensure that their new "improved
formula" was acceptable to consumer palates. And, indeed, it
was. In the short term, this fact-based approach helped coffee
companies offer a commercially viable product that consumers didn't reject outright. And the tests were right. Sales were
booming and profits were healthy. But the test data was hiding
a darker trend.

In 1964, coffee sales declined for the first time in the history
of the United States. At first, companies weren't sure what had
happened. Testing showed that long-time coffee drinkers were
satisfied with the product. However, this didn't tell the whole
story. Coffee drinkers weren't getting any younger. Any healthy
consumer business depends on attracting new generations of
customers to replace the old. And that wasn't happening. The
small additions of Robusta each year had quickly added up to
a lot of Robusta in the latest blends. If you had been drinking
coffee for years, the taste of a high-Robusta blend seemed perfectly tolerable. But if you had never drunk coffee in your life,
a cup made with Robusta seemed like a bitter and unpleasant
way to start the day. Young people, in particular, couldn't understand why their parents were hooked on such a foul drink. Sales
continued to decline as substitutes like Coke and Pepsi started
to make inroads. Coffee had turned into a low-growth, low-
margin business. Since focus groups had proven that the quality

of their products was good, executives presumed that young people were just responding to the packaging and advertising of the soda companies. The major coffee companies began to invest heavily in snappier marketing. But none of their efforts seemed to turn the tide.

It's important to note that coffee companies had relied on some very good maps to make their decisions. Marketers had paid careful attention to the expressed preferences of their consumers, and multiple studies insisted that people were unwilling to pay more for a cup of coffee. And multiple tests had proven that coffee drinkers couldn't tell the difference between the existing blend and one with more Robusta beans in it. What those consumer tests failed to show was an obvious truth: Independent of any incremental comparison, the coffee tasted bad. It also failed to show that people would be willing to pay a little more for good coffee if the companies only gave them a reason to do so. The map was not the territory.

The coffee business stayed focused on cost-cutting and additions of Robusta for decades, until someone decided to change the game. As it turns out, the market for high-quality Arabica coffee never completely went away. It survived as a niche business in small cafes located largely in urban centers and university towns. Things remained this way until a young entrepreneur named Howard Schultz visited Italy in the early 1980s and saw how espresso bars put coffee into a completely new light. People were perfectly willing to spend more for a good cup of coffee if the difference in quality was made clear to them. Returning to the States, Schultz was sure of one thing: The maps were wrong. At his new company, Starbucks, he built a chain of espresso bars that were focused on brewing premium quality coffee drinks. He provided a great experience to his customers. And little by little, his sustained success has pushed the American coffee industry to completely overhaul its approach. Starting in the 1990s, most coffee companies switched back to serving pure Arabica. A new generation of coffee drinkers got just as hooked on java as their parents once were.

GOING WITH YOUR GUT

The experience of American coffee companies highlights the challenge that any large organization faces in dealing with simplified information. The entire industry bet its future on abstract data from consumer tests. And because those tests produced quantitative results, they carried an air of authority that overruled any doubts about the use of Robusta in premium coffee blends. The industry was so focused on existing coffee drinkers that it unknowingly put itself into a death spiral. Every one of the managers involved in the degradation of American coffee knew that the products they were creating didn't taste good, but the companies made worse and worse coffee because their tests told them that the public wouldn't notice the difference. Lacking any real empathy, coffee executives became disconnected from their customers and fell for the lure of an attractive map.

In any organization, decision makers often find themselves working with simplified data that lacks any sort of context. They often deal with information in the abstract instead of experiencing it for themselves. In many cases, their disconnection from customers forces them to rely on so-called authorities who are anything but. Having an intuitive understanding of other people can help overcome these challenges. Empathy for the people you serve can make the abstract more grounded and immediate because that information is now connected to a real person you know. It can provide context for the data we receive by incorporating factors left off the map. And an empathic connection to other people can, over time, provide the kind of deep experience in a territory that people inside an organization need to identify new opportunities. In some cases, empathy can even keep a company from being torn apart.

GERSTNER DEFIES THE ANALYSTS

Lou Gerstner is a short, stocky man with salt-and-pepper hair and a warm, dignified smile. Always composed and collected, he speaks his mind plainly and with conviction. When Gerstner walks into a room, he exudes trustworthiness, confidence, and competence to everyone around him. Based on first impressions alone, Lou Gerstner strikes you as the kind of person you'd want running a large corporation.

His resume backs up that first impression. With a bachelor's degree in engineering from Dartmouth and an MBA from Harvard, Gerstner spent his formative years in business at McKinsey and Company, the famed management consultancy. Gerstner then served as president of American Express and dramatically grew its business, from 8.6 million to 30.7 million cardholders. After eleven years at American Express, he left to become chairman and chief executive officer of RJR Nabisco, where he successfully unified two disparate cultures that had been brought together in a difficult merger. He had deep experience in strategy and management, and he knew what worked when marketing to consumers. In every respect, Lou Gerstner was an ideal CEO for a large consumer packaged goods company.

Which made it all the more strange when Gerstner was selected to become CEO of IBM in 1993. At the time, the technology giant had found itself struggling to compete against more nimble competitors. IBM's core mainframe computer business seemed headed for obsolescence. Its cost structures were out of control. The company needed a strong leader if it were to survive. But critics doubted that Gerstner could fit the bill. In the tech industry, CEOs tend to follow one of two paths to the top. Either they cut their teeth in engineering, like Larry Ellison of Oracle, or they come up through sales and marketing, like Steve Ballmer at Microsoft. Gerstner didn't fit either model. For one thing, Gerstner had no background in technology. He was actually a bit of a technophobe. For another, Gerstner's experience was largely in selling to consumers, not in the business-to-business sales that were IBM's bread and butter. The business press questioned whether a guy who ran a cookie maker was capable of running the largest computer company in the world.

Others came out in Gerstner's favor, arguing that perhaps what IBM really needed was a great manager, not another tech guy. If nothing else, having a good manager at the helm might help IBM through the process of systematically dismantling the company. The conventional wisdom was that IBM could no longer compete as a single firm. Analysts, journalists, and industry leaders all agreed that only specialty-focused players could win in technology. Microsoft made only software. Intel made only microprocessors. Oracle made only business database software. IBM couldn't compete in an ecosystem of nimbler niche players. To survive, Big Blue needed to be broken up into a dozen Baby Blues. Nearly everyone who knew anything about the computer business agreed with this plan. Gerstner's predecessor, John Akers, had bought into this notion wholeheartedly and had already taken initial steps to break up the company. The storage unit was set to become Adstar. The printer business had been spun off as Lexmark. Everyone agreed that splitting up IBM was the right thing to do.

Everyone, that is, except Lou Gerstner. Just as people were getting used to the new guy from Nabisco, Gerstner announced that he intended to keep IBM together. Flying in the face of mounting judgment against IBM's outdated business model, Gerstner said IBM's greatest strength was its size and breadth. IBM could certainly be made to run leaner and meaner. Although that likely meant layoffs, it didn't have to mean breaking up the company. Gerstner later recalled, "It would have been insane to destroy its unique competitive advantage and turn IBM into a group of individual component suppliers—mere minnows in the ocean." Survival would depend on holding the company together.

The press disagreed wildly. Many business journalists openly questioned his competence to run IBM, regardless of his management pedigree. *Barron's* called Gerstner's strategy of slimming the company's staff without selling off business units "corporate anorexia." *The Economist* went further, saying investors might soon wish "that their axeman would turn visionary overnight."

Gerstner was undeterred. Though every analyst and even many of IBM's own managers had maps indicating that a breakup was the only answer, Gerstner ignored them. He intuitively sensed that IBM had a unique advantage against niche players in its ability to meld together solutions for its customers and deploy those solutions on a global scale. To drive this message home, IBM launched a new ad campaign. In a series of spots created by advertising powerhouse Ogilvy & Mather, people all over the world talked about how IBM was meeting their technology needs, from nuns in the Czech Republic to senior citizens in Paris. Clever and a little off-beat, the ads reinforced the idea that IBM's sheer size was its greatest strength. The folks in the ads didn't need a single PC—they all had special needs for a solution combining hardware, software, service, and support. More important, the campaign emphasized IBM as a global player, able to serve people from Beijing to Berlin. Introducing the slogan "Solutions for a small planet," Gerstner took IBM's most derided aspect—its enormous scale—and made it the company's singular competitive advantage.

The "Small Planet" campaign reintroduced IBM to the public as a global organization that could make technology work for business. While the new ads were being launched, Gerstner was revamping the company from the inside out. When he arrived, the company had been divided according to geographic region, which hampered IBM's capability to serve global customers. Gerstner restructured the company into divisions based on industries, not location, which created several new global groups capable of creating solutions for real business problems. He restructured management. He restructured marketing. He changed how employees and executives were compensated and incentivized.

Little by little, IBM started to turn the corner. During his first year on the job, Gerstner stopped the company's bleeding. By his second year, IBM was back to profitable growth across multiple new categories. In 1996, he repositioned IBM as an organization specializing in "e-business," capable of helping any company leverage the power of the Internet. By the time Gerstner stepped down in 2002, IBM was on top again. Moreover, the company's focus on solutions helped it build a remarkably profitable services and consulting business. IBM's revenues and profits grew every single year after Gerstner first took the job.

Looking back, perhaps the press was half-right. Maybe all IBM needed was a great manager. Gerstner broke up dysfunctional fiefdoms, slashed operating costs, and streamlined decision making. Along the way, he placed smart strategic bets on new technologies and emerging markets that helped drive topline growth. Though Gerstner was, indeed, a great manager, that description missed the bigger story. What the press didn't see when it predicted his failure was that he was something far more special than a great manager: Lou Gerstner was a real IBM customer. And more than his management style, strategic thinking, or motivational skills, it was Gerstner's experience as a customer that helped him understand the territory and save IBM. What Gerstner brought to the table was his empathy for IBM's customers.

At American Express, Gerstner had seen how his business's need for information technology had increased exponentially. Access to real-time information was crucial to ensuring that Amex charge cards worked wherever and whenever its members wanted to make a purchase. That required an ever-more complex system of computers, software, and telecommunications equipment. It required a massive global information infrastructure. American Express was unequipped to handle that sort of under-taking on its own. Fortunately, it was exactly the kind of problem that IBM tackled all the time. Gerstner had relied upon Big Blue to ensure that technology wouldn't fail American Express members. IBM built data centers, created custom software, and helped Amex develop global communication tools to keep the organization up and running. A dozen mini IBMs would never have been able to deliver the kind of service he relied upon at American Express. That's why, when the prevailing wisdom was dead set on breaking IBM apart, Gerstner stood his ground. As he noted, "The idea that all this complicated, difficult-to-integrate, proprietary collection of technologies was going to be purchased by customers who would be willing to be their own general contractors made no sense."

Gerstner knew about more than just the unique solutions IBM could offer its customers. He also understood the harm IBM could do to them because he had seen IBM at its worst. While he led American Express, one of Gerstner's division managers had purchased a single computer from Amdahl to test in his huge, IBM-based data center. When IBM found out about the purchase, it retaliated like an enraged child, canceling all support for the millions of dollars of IBM hardware and software contained in the data center and alienating one of IBM's biggest customers in the process. As Gerstner saw it, such nonsense had no place at IBM. Big Blue would be a company that cared about its number-one customers: corporate executives in large companies who depended on technology to make their businesses work.

That caring translated into an almost fanatical interest in what business customers had to say about IBM. Early in his tenure, Gerstner met with the CEOs of his top customers and asked them to tell him about all that IBM was doing wrong. He learned that the products were far too expensive. The company's responsiveness was poor. IBM was spending tens of millions of dollars to send representatives to make in-person sales calls but then did a poor job of following up for support and service down the road. As a result, Gerstner focused company resources on responsiveness, price reduction, and support and services. The first two areas addressed problems with IBM that needed to be fixed. Support and services became a major growth area for the company. For the long term, Gerstner passed his attention to customers on to his top managers, obsessively asking them in every staff meeting, "What are you hearing from customers?" Forget about the technical details, what are the people saying out there? Gerstner reshaped IBM's culture to one of customer engagement. He worked to discover both what needed fixing about IBM today and which new markets to pursue down the road.

Throughout all this change, Gerstner spoke frequently with his most important customers to explain how his management changes and IBM's latest technologies could help solve their most pressing issues. He became a special kind of CEO: the chief explaining officer. Though he didn't always understand the nuance of how "CMOS technology" worked, he always did a great job explaining to his customers that it meant IBM mainframes would drop in price from $63,000 to $2,500 in a few short years. He wasn't a technologist, but he believed in the strategic power of information technology, so he did a good job explaining the value of IT to other business leaders.

In keeping IBM together, Lou Gerstner defied the advice of Wall Street analysts, competitors, and even some of his own lieutenants. He was able to transcend a barrage of bad information because he possessed contextual knowledge that others lacked: the experience of being an IBM customer. The existence of category specialists like Oracle and Intel wasn't an argument to break up the company. On the contrary, it was *because* there were so many specialty players that an integrator was needed. Corporate customers simply didn't want to get into the business of designing their own multiplatform technology solutions. In light of this obvious truth, breaking up IBM would have been a catastrophically poor decision. Gerstner was one of the few people who could see that, because he knew what life was really like for IBM's customers. After all, he'd been one of them.

THE QUESTION OF IMMEDIACY

The contextual knowledge that led Lou Gerstner to keep IBM together is what people often call street smarts or gut sense. It's an intuitive understanding of the realities on the ground. And it's what great leaders often depend on. Having an informed intuition can help decision makers transcend conventional wisdom and see opportunities that others can't. That's the primary benefit of empathy—it's a gut sense for what's going on in other people's lives. When that empathic connection with customers exists, it can help leaders to know what matters most to the people who drive sales. Empathy is the antidote for the simplified, abstract information that often carries authority inside organizations. Empathy helps people see the world as it really is, not how it looks on a map.

Few maps provide the level of immediacy that's necessary to accurately convey what's happening on the ground in the territories they represent. This is a problem. To be truly useful to a business, any map of a market doesn't just need to depict the data; it must convey an accurate picture of the people who live, work, and play in that market. It must allow the people reading the map to accurately imagine what life might be like if they were to be part of that territory. Unless they can really understand what a territory looks, sounds, and feels like, decision makers will struggle to accurately interpret their own maps.

MAKING ABSTRACTIONS TANGIBLE

Joe Rohde understands the value of immediacy. Rohde is an Imagineer, part of Disney's research and development arm. He's also a world traveler and is famous in the organization for visiting the least-developed places on the planet to get a clear picture of the parts of life that people in America miss out on. During his travels, Rohde saw that Disney had an opportunity to do something spectacular with wild animals. He envisioned a safari-like experience that would allow you to feel the rumble of parading elephants to your left and the quake of a lion's roar on your right. Disney could create the ultimate adventure in the wild that would be compelling because it was immersive and authentic.

There was only one problem. Disney didn't do zoos. At multiple points in the company's history, executives had considered the idea, only to come back with the same conclusions: Zoos were boring, depressing places. Animals didn't make for compelling content. Fantasy was simply much more interesting than reality. If he was going to succeed, Rohde needed to overcome this bias. He decided to make an impassioned pitch to Disney's board for what he called the Animal Kingdom, a theme park filled with wild creatures and exciting rides. His team would transform a portion of central Florida into a safari unlike any other. In the presentation, Rohde answered skeptical questions about development costs and guest traffic. He showed that the project could make money. But there was still the zoo thing. During the discussion, CEO Michael Eisner fundamentally questioned the idea that looking at animals would get people excited. "They're just animals," he wondered aloud. "So what?"

"I thought you might say that," Rohde said, smiling. Rohde got up from his chair and walked over to the door of Eisner's office. He opened it to reveal a 400-pound Bengal tiger. A team of handlers led the tiger into the room and over toward a stunned Eisner. The Disney chairman had never been this close to a beast of such proportions. This thing was bigger than a desk. The tiger brushed her massive head against the CEO's body and growled in low rumbles, shaking the once sedate office. "I see your point," Eisner said. In a second, he was able to understand how wild animals could be thrilling attractions for vacationing families. He finally got what Rohde had been talking about for so long. Eisner decided to approve Disney's Animal Kingdom.

Following its launch in 1998, the Animal Kingdom quickly became one of the world's most popular theme parks, drawing 8.9 million visitors per year, with tickets starting at $70 a person. Whether you've seen a live tiger in your office or not, you can understand why Disney finds a half-billion dollars of incremental revenue to be compelling. The park's success is a testament to what can be lost when business is performed solely in the abstract. Building a zoo made no sense on paper for Disney. In the real world, however, it was a bold new opportunity. Only the immediate thrill of an actual wild animal encounter could make Michael Eisner see how the Animal Kingdom might connect with people. He needed to be put in the shoes of someone who would someday visit the park. To see the value of the proposal, Eisner needed to be shown the territory.

ALTERNATIVES TO USING A TIGER

When people are asked to evaluate an idea in the abstract, they often lack the data required to make a good decision. Abstractions of reality are easy to digest, but they can't tell the whole story, which can get people into trouble. If Eisner hadn't been confronted by a growling tiger, he would have dismissed the Animal Kingdom proposal as just another zoo. After all, the proposal only summarized what the real experience might be like. But Joe Rohde made his map of a Disney safari park tangible for Eisner, and the promise of his concept was immediately clear. Disney was able to act on the opportunity and add a wildly popular attraction to the company's portfolio.

Making abstractions tangible can provide the immediacy needed for leaders to imagine themselves in the shoes of the people they serve. Such activities can take any number of forms, most of which are a lot easier to arrange than a guest appearance by a wild animal. Decision makers who seek to transcend abstractions learn to spend time with the people they serve. They shop where their customers shop. They visit with them in their homes. They go out of their way to experience life as their customers do. All this is in the hopes of gathering contextual knowledge for the decisions they make. In doing so, effective decision makers feed their heads with multisensory information to reveal the meaning behind the data.

THE COST OF NOT KNOWING THE TERRITORY

Empathy can provide decision makers with context, a clear sense of the implications of what they're seeing, as Lou Gerstner showed at IBM. It can add life to otherwise unremarkable data, as Michael Eisner's encounter with a tiger did. Without this context and immediacy, it's nearly impossible to interpret new data. It's difficult to evaluate the credibility of a map if you've never been to the territory.

In the wake of the September 11th attacks, the airline industry found itself in deep trouble. Delta Airlines was one of the major carriers forced to slash costs just to survive. Having survived that troubled period, Delta then started to consider new ways to grow. A research team was assembled and charged with the task of studying the flying experience. Intuitively, the team knew that there were huge opportunities for making the experience better for passengers. And they believed that people were willing to pay for a better experience. Knowing something, however, is quite different from proving it. The team knew it needed data to back up its assertions if it hoped to win the support of upper management. The team decided to spend several hundred thousand dollars to catalog how air travelers felt about flying. The results were as expected. With security checks, delays, and poor service, flying in America was a dreadful experience. The report made this point plainly. In detail, it laid out everything that could—and, indeed, should—be fixed about flying if Delta wanted to grow in an increasingly competitive marketplace.

It was, therefore, surprising to the researchers when Delta's senior management rejected the report. In the executives' minds, air travel was fine, especially given how little Americans had to pay for a ticket. Stories of lousy service, air rage, and irate passengers were nothing more than media hype. Such an assertion seems patently ludicrous to anyone who doesn't work in the airline industry. But that's how Delta leadership saw the world. Of course, such a disconnect isn't surprising when you consider what it was like to work as an executive at Delta. The airline's headquarters is located in Atlanta, right next to Hartsfield–Jackson International Airport. If a Delta executive needed to make a flight, his assistant would call for a shuttle to pick him up in front of the building. The shuttle would then drive onto the tarmac, taking him directly to his gate. The executive then needed only to climb a few steps up to the Jetway and walk straight into first class. As one Delta employee noted, most senior managers had never seen the inside of an economy class cabin. Little wonder, then, that Delta executives thought flying was great. It was…for them.

Delta is not alone in having leaders who are disconnected from the world. Many companies facing a tough market refuse to make decisions that can't be backed up by facts. Yet it's hard to tell good facts from bad when your own experience of the world is too narrow. The twentieth century gave rise to an extraordinary collection of tools and systems that allow companies to quickly assess the performance and direction of their businesses. These maps are rooted in authoritative, provable science, and they simplify the world into a set of relevant data. They also leave out the most important parts of any business—rich, implicit information about the people that a company serves. Empathy can solve that. Learning to empathically connect with customers can go a long way toward helping businesses prosper in the long term. This is not a radically new idea, but it has the potential to improve how companies perform. In fact, it's the way all business used to be done.

THREE

The Way Things Used to Be

*Empathy isn't a new phenomenon. There was
a time not so long ago when there was a broad
and deep connection between producers and
consumers that allowed everyone to prosper.*

MY COLLEAGUES AND I teach a class at Stanford called Needfinding. The class is about using social research methods for design. In it, we teach design and business school students how to get out into the world and observe people, and then analyze their observations to discover unmet needs. We teach them how to spend time with people, learn about their lives, and then make better products and businesses as a result. The first day of the class is largely about logistics, distributing handouts and putting things in place so we can get going. Day two is Play-Doh Day.

At the beginning of class, we ask students to sit next to the person they know best. Many of the students have been in the same classes together for a few years. A few are even roommates. We hand out cans of Play-Doh to every team. The assignment is fairly straightforward. Every student is asked to create a utensil to help their partner eat their favorite food. They usually have about twenty minutes to complete the task. As the class goes about the exercise, I like to wander through the room and watch how different students go about solving the problem.

Most of the students start off by asking their partner what their favorite food is. They then make some nifty gadget that they think will improve the experience. For example, one person might say that they like pizza, so their partner makes a knife with a pizza wheel on the end to cut off little pieces. Many of these teams tend to have a quick discussion to get some information and then spend the rest of the time working separately on their utensil. Other students take advantage of the fact that Play-Doh is incredibly easy to shape and reshape. They first have a conversation about what kind of food each person likes and then mock up something quickly to get feedback from their partner. That sparks another conversation about what their partner likes or dislikes about the utensil, which gets them working on a revised version. They might make fifteen different utensils in the course of twenty minutes, and they often end up with a finished idea that looks nothing like what they expected to make when they started out. These students really understand the value of rapid prototyping. Yet another group of students takes a completely different approach. They don't do a whole lot of trial and revision, but they carry on a conversation with each other while they work. Some of what they talk about might be the food that they eat. Most of it is just shooting the breeze while they work.

When time is up, we go around the room and share what everyone came up with. I ask students to tell us who their partner was, what their favorite food is, and what they ended up making. Invariably, each of the different approaches yields very different results. The first type of students, the ones who worked in relative isolation, often make some very novel stuff. I remember one student, in particular, who created an elegant utensil to hold fried chicken. When I asked his partner if she would ever actually use something like that, she shrugged her shoulders and said she really liked to eat chicken with her hands, so probably not. A lot of the really novel ideas seem to get that kind of reaction. By contrast, students who do a lot of prototyping usually come up with ideas that their partners like better. Working with someone who likes spaghetti, a student might begin with a noodle twirler before realizing that his partner really needs some sort of sauce splash-guard instead. This group's success makes sense; their partners essentially help in the design.

The last group of students, the ones who looked like they were shooting the breeze and wasting time, often ends up with the most surprises. They're the most likely to solve a need that their partners didn't know they had. For instance, one student created an anti-dribble spoon to help his buddy eat Cheerios. He explained that his partner always dribbled milk down his chin when he ate, so this spoon would prevent him from staining his shirt. I asked his partner if he dribbled, and he sternly denied the accusation. "No way," he said. "Sure you do," his friend responded. "I've been sitting across from you at breakfast for four years now, and you always dribble. You might not see it, but trust me, you need it!"

At the end of the exercise, I ask each group how long they've known each other. Invariably, the longer a team has known each other, the better they do. The folks who've worked in isolation often turn out to have known no one else in the class, so when they sat next to the person they knew the "best," it was someone they had just met. The teams with the most provocative designs have often lived together for years, like our Cheerios dribbler and his buddy did. Those students often know little secrets about each other that lead to solutions that wouldn't be possible otherwise.

I assign the Play-Doh exercise for several reasons. First, our class is a design class, so it's good to start by making things.

Second, it's a good illustration of how understanding other people can lead to interesting new solutions. Third and most important, I want students to realize that this is how most things got made for most of human history. For thousands of years, people made things for other people they knew. Tailors stitched clothes for their friends and family. Cobblers made shoes for people who lived down the street. That intimacy helped a cobbler know whether you had flat feet, liked to walk, or sprained your ankle last summer. All of that ended when something transformative happened to human society: a rift grew between producers and consumers that we've been struggling to repair ever since.

THE RISE OF THE INDUSTRIAL REVOLUTION

The economic history of the world over the last five thousand years can be summarized as a flat horizontal line. For millennia, the total per capita productivity of the world remained essentially the same. The population increased, but we produced and consumed the same amount of stuff per person. Then, around the year 1800, we had growth. Exponential, cascading growth. Technological, political, and economic change transformed society. In the 200 years since then, productivity per capita in the world's richest economies has increased to 12 times the historic norm. This wasn't a slight disruption. It was the economic equivalent of repealing the laws of gravity.

The Industrial Revolution created wealth on a scale the world had never seen. The beneficiaries of this revolution were profoundly transformed. Between 1760 and 1860, the population of Great Britain tripled. Life expectancy nearly doubled. Infant mortality rates plunged to less than a tenth of their historic norm. Nonfarm output increased tenfold. Between 1820 and 1900, England changed from a country where 45 percent of the population could read to one where 95 percent of the population was literate. National networks of railroads were constructed, enabling more rapid trade and tourism. Steamships increased the speed and reduced the cost of overseas shipping. This massive transformation left behind a legacy of essential public institutions, economic prosperity, and social change throughout much of the industrialized world.

The Industrial Revolution had global reach. Great Britain's economy switched from one with almost no net exports to one in which 20 percent of its Gross Domestic Product came from sales to other nations. New trade routes opened up as cheap, innovative goods were shipped around the world to new customers in new markets. Imports and exports both increased as dense populations in London, New York, and Chicago became unable to feed themselves, yet able to trade a surplus of manufactured goods for other regions' surplus food. The middle class expanded. For the first time in human history, the place of your birth started to become less important than your ability to work hard and commercialize new opportunities. You could live anywhere, sell anywhere, and travel anywhere. Reaching a customer thousands of miles from home was suddenly a possibility. Constraints that had defined commerce for thousands of years shrank or vanished.

THE RIFT BETWEEN PRODUCERS AND CONSUMERS

For all of the Industrial Revolution's wonderful impacts on the ability of the average person to go into business, it also created a giant rift between producers and consumers. Nearly overnight, we went from a world of face-to-face commercial transactions to a world that was simultaneously more connected and further apart. Today, we make things for people we've never met.

The United States has a gross domestic product of more than $13 trillion, including more than $1 trillion in exports. More than 60 percent of those exports travel beyond North America, reaching markets and people that Americans know little about. We also import about $2 trillion worth of goods per year, more than 70 percent of it arriving from outside North America. This gulf between producers and consumers is mirrored around the world. Japanese companies sell electronics and cars to Europe and the United States, who export their own cars to each other; India and China dominate manufacturing for soft and hard goods worldwide. India has pioneered techniques for software development and customer management that don't require its people to ever see a customer firsthand. As a result, few producers have a clear picture of what life is really like for the people who buy their products. It's as if we're all playing the Play-Doh game with people who live on the other side of the planet, creating utensils to help them eat a food we've often never tasted ourselves.

Consider the example of the Tubbs Snowshoe Company. If you're looking to go on a winter hike through deep snow, you might want to get a pair of Tubbs snowshoes. They're light, strong, and they look great, too. Tubbs owner Ed Kiniry first produced the metal snowshoes in 1987, back when everyone else was making old-fashioned wooden shoes. Tubbs snowshoes used to be made in the tiny resort town of Stowe, Vermont, by folks who loved to spend time outdoors in the snow. Today, the shoes are made in Guangzhou, China, by workers who see snow about as often as a blizzard strikes Miami Beach. It turns out that in 2004, Kiniry sold Tubbs to K2, a large sports equipment company well known for its skis. K2 moved snowshoe production to its manufacturing complex in Guangzhou. Located near the South China Sea, Guangzhou is an industrial city larger than Los Angeles. The weather tends to be hot and humid in the summer and dry and mild in the winter. It's about as far away from snowshoe country as you can get.

It should be noted that the factory in Guangzhou makes snowshoes that are every bit as good as the ones that were made in Vermont. But something has been lost when snowshoes are made by people who've never seen snow. It's unclear how workers in the Guangzhou complex can know whether the shoes they make are any good. While K2's designers and executives reside in cooler regions and have a sense for snow sports, the company has lost any sort of frontline feedback to make up for leaders' blind spots. Workers at the Guangzhou facility don't have great intuition for how to improve the snowshoes they work on every day. They'll probably never come up with a radically new direction for the industry the way Vermont native Ed Kiniry did when he improved on the old wooden designs. None of this is to say that employees at the K2 facility aren't creative or don't want to make things better. They're simply so far removed from their customers that they have the deck stacked against them.

The challenges facing the makers of Tubbs Snowshoes going forward reflect an important truth of the global economy: It's much harder to succeed when you create things for people you don't know and whose lives seem alien to your own. When companies make products for people who live far away from them, they often make silly mistakes in their design and marketing. These mistakes are caused at least in part by linguistic and cultural differences. Americans who don't speak Swedish are more likely to accidentally select a funny or offensive name for their Swedish products. Not so long ago, one of the largest manufacturers of men's underwear in China considered entering the U.S. market only to find that Pansy brand underwear wouldn't exactly click with American men!

Before the Industrial Revolution, it was fairly easy to guess which products would sell well. Producers and consumers led similar lives and shared tremendous implicit knowledge about each other. The broader the reach of individual companies has become, the more that this implicit connection between producer and consumer has diminished. Manufacturing managers in Guangzhou don't intuitively know what life is like for someone who loves to snowshoe. Brand managers in Battle Creek, Michigan, have little sense for what children in New Delhi want for breakfast. Engineers in Silicon Valley create computer software for retirees in Palm Beach without any sense of what it's like to be older. Marketers in financial services companies are unfamiliar with the everyday challenges facing the rural poor who sign up for their car loans. Companies don't know their customers on a personal level, so they struggle to create and market products that resonate with ordinary folks. Leaders are left to conclude that they can't accurately predict the success or failure of any individual initiative without sophisticated testing. Despite living in an age where technology has made always-on data connections ubiquitous, we are more disconnected from the people we impact than at any other time in human history.

Though immediacy in commerce has become a rare commodity, it hasn't gone away altogether. Moreover, we still crave it. Fortunate is the company that knows its customers as real people. We all prefer to buy products from businesses that show real knowledge of our needs. And people who understand how their work plays a positive role in the lives of their customers produce better results and feel better about it, too. Creating greater empathy within the business world could have many different outcomes, from positive social change to greater revenue growth. Of all the possible results, however, this one is most certain: Empathy can help draw producers and consumers together, and heal the rift that began with the Industrial Revolution. To better understand what that looks like, I decided to visit one of the oldest companies in the world. For nearly 400 years, it has maintained a closeness to the people it serves that has transcended any kind of market research or customer testing. The result is a relationship that has stood the test of time.

STAYING CLOSE TO DRUMMERS

If you play the drums, there's a monument to your craft, and it's located about twenty miles southeast of Boston. There, in an unassuming factory in Norwell, Massachusetts, the Avedis Zildjian Company creates what are undeniably the best cymbals in the world. Inside the company's walls are memorabilia from the most famous drummers of all time, including Gene Krupa, Buddy Rich, Steve Gadd, and Ringo Starr. Autographed photos of famous musicians line the walls. Framed gold and platinum records hang as gifts of appreciation from top-tier artists. Buddy Rich's old drum kit stands as a gatekeeper to a special lounge where marquee artists try out the latest equipment and select particular cymbals to call their own. No matter whether your tastes run to jazz, rock, hip hop, or classical music, Zildjian is the gold standard.

Zildjian is a peculiar name for a family-owned business in Massachusetts. Indeed, the Zildjian story actually began outside Istanbul, Turkey, in the year 1618. There, in the small town of Samatya, a young Armenian alchemist named Avedis was working in his laboratory. Like a lot of very bright but misguided men of his era, he was trying to make gold from base metals. Avedis had constructed a laboratory in the hopes of getting rich quickly. Yet unlike so many of his contemporaries, Avedis actually discovered something amazing. In the course of a prolonged series of experiments, he developed an alloy of copper, tin, and silver that had a most surprising property: It bounced. Most bronze castings fall on the ground with a heavy thud when they're dropped. The alloy that Avedis had created bounced like a ball. That alone made the alloy an oddity, but it also had another interesting property. When the metal bounced, it rang like a bell.

Fascinated by the sound of the new alloy, and more than a bit discouraged with his own ability to turn lead into gold, Avedis began to fashion the metal into cymbals. At the time, cymbals were used primarily by the military. The Ottoman Army used cymbals as a means of psychological warfare, creating loud crashes to intimidate its enemies. Avedis's cymbals created resonant crashes unlike any other. Delighted with his creation, Avedis set out for Istanbul to seek an audience with Murad IV, Sultan of the Ottoman Empire. When the sultan finally agreed to see him, he was amazed by the power and clarity of the new cymbals. These were cymbals that would strike fear into his enemies' troops, even as they inspired his own. He placed a large order with Avedis and quickly followed with requests for more. He ordered the cymbals to be played at weddings and affairs of state. He covered Avedis in gold and fame and eventually bestowed upon him the title of Zildjian, meaning Maker of Cymbals. The family dynasty was born, and Avedis built a cymbal factory near his home in Samatya. Working with his sons and neighbors, Avedis would heat up castings of his secret alloy to 1,600 degrees Fahrenheit and then cool them down with salt-water carried from the nearby Sea of Marmara. Avedis hammered, shaped, buffed, and delivered cymbal after cymbal to the court of the Ottoman Empire.

For the next 300 years, Avedis' descendants would continue to create cymbals based on the family's secret alloy. Composers began to write music that called for cymbals. Mozart peppered his scores with cymbal parts. The German composer Nicolaus Strungk was so astounded by the power of Zildjian cymbals that he wrote his opera, *Esther*, around the sound—and even asked for Zildjians by name. The Zildjian family capitalized on this interest and worked hard to ensure that they had a tight bond with both composers and musicians. In the 1850s, Avedis II built a schooner to sail cymbals to musicians in Western Europe. His brother, Kerope, traveled far and wide to promote the family's name. He won awards at trade fairs around the globe: Paris, Vienna, Bologna, Chicago, and Boston. These trips were more than sales calls. They were an important way for the Zildjian family to meet artists in person and learn firsthand about how music was evolving.

Zildjian continued to prosper until the turn of the twentieth century, when Turkey ceased to be a welcome home for Armenians. Like many prosperous minorities throughout history, Armenians had come to be viewed with hostility by the Turkish majority. An Armenian nationalist movement only fed the flames of suspicion and jealousy among Turks. Growing tensions led to a brutal crackdown. The government seized Armenian land. Many Armenians were arrested indiscriminately. European observers estimated that at least 100,000 Armenians were killed between 1894 and 1896 under the tacit approval of the Ottoman government. Even a family as well known as the Zildjians found themselves on the run. Aram Zildjian, the head of the family, decided to move his company to Bucharest.

There the Zildjian Company stayed, until Aram's young nephew set out for Boston in 1908. Having decided that he wanted nothing to do with the family business, Avedis Zildjian III left to seek his fortune in America. Picking up work at a Boston candy factory, Avedis learned every aspect of the business, from manufacturing to delivery to finance. Avedis eventually got married and had five children with his wife, Sally. He was even able to set up a candy company of his own. And that would have been the end of the story, except that, one day in 1927, Avedis got a letter in the mail.

"My dear nephew," the letter started. "It is with happiness, sorrow, and deep concern that I write this letter. The time has come when failing health will soon make it impossible for me to continue making the cymbals for which our family has been famous for over 300 years. For you, the son of my late brother, Haroushan, I am happy. Except for me, you are the oldest living male member in the Zildjian family. As such, you are next in line to become heir to the family's secret formula, the process for making cymbals which has been the pride of the Zildjian family for centuries. It now becomes your responsibility to take over the secret that is your heritage. Aram."

Avedis was shocked and dismayed. As far as he was concerned, he had left the family legacy behind in the old world, nearly two decades before. He had a new business, and there was no way he would get sucked back into the family craft. Candy was a going concern—cymbals were a dying industry! Nevertheless, it wouldn't be easy to reject his uncle's request. Aram was a tall, 300-pound man with a bald head, a white goatee, and a personality that seemed larger than life. What's more, he and two cymbal-making assistants were already on their way to Boston. At the end of the day, Avedis didn't have much of a choice.

Into the tranquil domestic life that Avedis and his family enjoyed, a giant from the East arrived, bearing the family secret. For two years, Aram and his assistants taught Avedis how to cast the family's bronze alloy, how to hammer molten castings into flat panels, and how to shape them into cymbals. Of course, making cymbals was only half the challenge. Avedis still had to sell them to someone, and he was half a world away from German composers and Ottoman Emperors. Sally convinced her husband to go to Boston's new jazz music clubs to see if any of the visiting drummers might be interested in buying some cymbals. Musicians from around the country regularly swung through Boston; why not ask them directly? To Avedis's great surprise, everyone he spoke with was hungry for better cymbals. At the time, all cymbals were optimized for use with orchestras, not drum kits. Worse, those unwieldy cymbals had to be imported from Europe and were nearly impossible to find.

Avedis began to form close relationships with the drummers he met. He'd hang out backstage with visiting musicians, talking for hours about how they played. As he soon discovered, jazz drummers needed far greater quantities and varieties of cymbals than other musicians did. The orchestral cymbals that Zildjian had made for years were simply too loud and heavy to use on a drum kit. They required drummers to muffle them with their hands, something that's hard to do when holding drumsticks. Talking late into the night, drummers like Gene Krupa, Papa Jo Jones, and Chick Webb filled Avedis's head with ideas for new products. Avedis set out to reinvent the cymbal.

The process was immediately fruitful. The drummers told him they wanted a cymbal that could make a dramatic impact and then disappear quickly, to match when the trumpets made a quick blast. In response, Avedis created a thinner cymbal that he called a Crash. Jazz legend Gene Krupa wanted a cymbal that he could use to keep time on, so Avedis designed a cymbal that didn't ring much, but provided a nice jingling chatter when you beat a rhythm on it. He called his creation the Ride cymbal, and like the Crash, it quickly became standard equipment for a drummer. Avedis would watch his friends perform, and then talk with them afterward. Paying close attention to their performances, Avedis revamped his entire product line to be suitable for jazz music. The resulting creations, the Crash, the Ride, the Splash, and the Hi-Hat, are all staples of the modern drum set. The strategy was so successful that the company was able to build a new factory in the midst of the Great Depression. In 1938, Avedis was featured in *Newsweek* magazine as one of America's master craftsmen, someone who was prospering despite the economic hard times.

The Avedis Zildjian Company grew steadily over the next several decades by always staying close to the drummers it served. Eventually, Avedis passed the secret formula of the Zildjian alloy on to his son Armand. Behind locked doors, Avedis showed his son the family's secret method for transforming copper and tin into castings of Zildjian bronze. As the young boy grew older, he became adept at every part of the cymbal-making process, from design, to forging, to finishing, to delivery. With practice, Armand became a master cymbal maker worthy of the name Zildjian.

Even as he mastered the art of cymbal making, Armand labored to learn the art of drumming, as well. While his father had loved to hang out with drummers, Armand became a drummer himself. He loved to stay out late and party with other musicians. No matter who was in Boston on a given weekend, Armand was a permanent fixture backstage. They would talk until three in the morning about life, drumming, and their hopes for the future. Ideas for new kinds of cymbals often came up in casual conversation, all of which Armand filed away for future reference. As Avedis passed the company to Armand in the 1970s, Zildjian's deep connections to drummers had helped make its cymbals the choice of not just jazz drummers, but of rock stars, too.

Armand combined his knowledge of cymbal making with his love for music. He revamped the company's cherished manufacturing process to produce a more consistent and even higher-quality product through technologies that maintained an artisan's care and touch. He created a soundproof lounge where visiting drummers could try out new cymbals and offer feedback on new prototypes. Frustrated that no one recognized the contributions that drummers had made to music, Armand founded the American Drummers' Achievement Awards to recognize the heroes of his craft. When he died in 2002, his passing was mourned by drummers and lovers of music around the world.

Today, the intuitive relationship that Armand enjoyed with drummers lives on. Zildjian is a place that actively seeks to connect with drummers and meet their individual needs, just as artisans have for millennia. By staying close to drummers, the company is never at a loss for where to take its product lines or its business. On countless occasions, Zildjian has used a direct request from a professional drummer as inspiration for its next big line of cymbals. In 1990, Vinnie Colaiuta was getting ready to play with Sting, so he asked for a cymbal with a modern, refined sound. The A Custom line, the company's all-time top-seller, was born. In 2006, Akira Jimbo, a Japanese drumming legend, had an idea for a cymbal that would be half-polished and half-unfinished, giving two different sounds on the same instrument. The wildly successful K Custom Hybrid line was born. Just as new artists make new kinds of music, Zildjian connects with new artists to help create new kinds of cymbals.

After almost 400 years, Zildjian remains the undisputed market leader in cymbals in both sales and quality. This couldn't have happened without Zildjian's deep connection to drummers. Many of the people who work at Zildjian are drummers, just like Armand. But an even larger number of folks are simply interested in making cymbals for musicians, just like Armand's father.

Zildjian succeeds the old-fashioned way. Instead of spending time on market research or R&D exploration, the company forms deep relationships with drummers and pays attention to what they need. Back in 1623, when the company was started, that's how all business was done. So close was the relationship between producers and consumers that a sultan could name a family for the product that it made. That's consumer-driven branding on a level that few companies will ever experience. When companies have an empathic connection with the people they serve, they're able to adjust to changing markets more effectively. They stay focused on what really matters, and they identify new opportunities more quickly. Empathy makes you nimble.

No one at Zildjian has trouble understanding who they really serve—it's the drummers. Unfortunately, this situation is quite uncommon. At many companies, only market researchers and sales representatives spend much, if any, time with customers. Other organizations engage with people only during focus groups and product testing. Even then, only a very small percentage of the organization directly meets with its customers. The insights they gather end up condensed into numbers on PowerPoint slides, and the people that those numbers represent slip out of view. Companies have become disconnected from their real customers, in exchange for reassuring figures like "59 percent of suburban fathers have favorable impressions of the brand." It's little wonder that managers end up feeling they have no control over the success or failure of new product launches. They spend so much time running the numbers that they've lost the ability to meet face to face with ordinary people.

This is not an irreversible situation. Many companies, such as Harley-Davidson and IBM, have already created practices that restore the implicit empathy for their customers that benefited artisans in bygone eras. These organizations take steps to be more like the people they're trying to serve, and their sustained growth is a testament to their success. They consciously cultivate empathy to guide their businesses. What these practices have in common is that they go to great lengths to make commerce more immediate, in contrast to the rest of the business world. They step outside themselves to directly gain experience of their customers' lives. To them, people are much more than a collection of facts. Companies benefit when they find ways to make the invisible facts of life more concrete, by getting outside and meeting the people that they might otherwise only read about in the newspaper or in a market research report. As they've learned, funny things happen when producers meet consumers: Their assumptions about each other get replaced by direct experience, and both sides profit from the encounter.

NINA PLANCK AND THE
LONDON FARMERS' MARKETS

For all intents and purposes, Nina Planck jumpstarted the urban farmers' market movement in Great Britain. She didn't really mean to kick off a resurgence in local food consumption, but that's how movements go sometimes. All Nina wanted to do was make the world she lived in look a little bit more like the one she grew up in. What Nina created in the process was a model for doing business that makes the commercial transaction far more immediate. The way things used to be.

It started one day in 1999 when Nina left her London home in search of carrots. She's a great cook, and she likes to work with the freshest of vegetables, the choicest of meats, and the ripest of fruits. And that day, she had a hankering for carrots. So Nina went to the market, marched in to the produce section and grabbed a bunch of carrots. She was about to put them in her basket and head for the check-out out when she read the label: "Product of France." Confused, she picked up another bunch. Same story. She checked the other vegetables. The peppers were from the Netherlands. The tomatoes were from Israel. The Granny Smith apples came all the way from New Zealand. Nina had just discovered a little-known secret of Britain's food supply: More than half of its vegetables are imported, and more than 95 percent of its fruit comes from overseas. "I was shocked," she said. "I couldn't buy local food anywhere."

This wasn't what Nina had expected to find when she left her home in America to move to Europe. She had awakened a few months earlier to find herself an adult with a real job who had somehow never been to Europe. As a cosmopolitan congressional staffer with a degree from Georgetown, Nina found this unacceptable. She needed to get to Europe right away. Nina soon found herself on a plane bound for Brussels, where a five-month-long internship at NATO awaited. Quickly falling for the quaint charms of the Old Country, Nina bounced around the continent a little bit before winding up in London as a speechwriter for the U.S. Ambassador to the United Kingdom. Life was good. Nina had close friends in London. She was making a living. She loved England even more than she had hoped she might.

But as her trip to the grocery store showed, something crucial was missing: local food, the kind she had grown up with on her parents' farm in Wheatland, Virginia. As a child, she had spent every weekend taking vegetables to sell at local farmers' markets. By the time she was nine, Nina was traveling to distant markets on her own to sell her family's fresh tomatoes, beans, squash, zukes, cukes, peppers, eggplant, corn, basil, flowers, strawberries, winter squash, spinach, collards, kale, lettuce, and garlic. "Basic truck farming stuff," Nina recalls. During peak season, the Planck family would set up at seventeen markets a week. They raised, harvested, transported, and sold all of their own food. By the age of 12, Nina had even started to run markets of her own.

Now a young woman in London, Nina was ready to bring her childhood experience of food to England. She knew that, run properly, farmers' markets could make small farms financially viable. So she decided to set up a market of her own. Nina began contacting farmers and inviting them to sell their goods at her new market. She had only two conditions: Their crops had to be grown within a hundred miles of London, and they could sell only what they grew themselves. This was a marked rebuttal to the complex supply chain needed to provide organic tomatoes from Israel to a shop on a London street corner. Instead of eight or more steps in between producer and consumer, Nina offered one. She called her idea the Wheatland Farmers' Market in honor of her home town.

Nina opened her market on June 6, 1999, in London's posh Islington neighborhood. The response was overwhelming. Curious visitors queued up in anticipation of the grand opening. Two serving cabinet ministers attended, and the minister of agriculture rang the opening bell. Prince Charles issued a statement to commend the market's arrival. When the gates opened, people nearly trampled each other trying to get at the locally produced fruits, vegetables, and meat. The farmers' stocks quickly ran out. Nina herself bought the last carrot. It turns out that she wasn't the only one who missed locally grown food. Within three months, Nina would open two more markets and quite happily quit her day job.

Now renamed London Farmers' Markets, Nina's company operates fourteen markets throughout London and offers food from more than 180 different producers. Nina has also launched a dozen markets in the United States. But beyond her company, she has also started a trend. When her first market opened in Islington, it was the first of its kind in London, and there were only 11 farmers' markets in all of Britain. Now there are more than 400 across the country. Nina's had quite a spectacular impact on the way people throughout England buy and eat fresh produce.

A CAPITALIST, NOT AN ACTIVIST

Nina's tale is an interesting chapter in the story of how eating is changing in the developed world. But it's also a powerful case study in the ongoing experiment called capitalism. Her farmers' markets did more than offer good veggies to upwardly mobile urbanites. They were a forum for bringing producers and consumers back together. That intimacy has acted as a sort of market accelerator to make sure that her shoppers get the best possible food and her farmers get the best possible prices. Interestingly, Nina's customers don't cite organic qualities, lack of hormones, or nutritional value to explain their interest in farmers' markets. They appreciate the quality of the food and the value they get for their money. But rather than rest on their laurels, her farmers understand that how ordinary people define "quality food" is continually changing as they learn more about where their food comes from.

As a result, Nina doesn't have to over-regulate the practices for her markets. She's never had to mandate organic growing practices, ban the use of growth hormones in livestock, or ask her growers not to use genetically modified crops. Her producers all chose to adopt those standards before she ever needed to think about enforcing them. That's what the customers right in front of them expected, and so they provided it.

Moreover, allowing market forces to dictate the adoption of cutting-edge practices makes such changes far more enduring for both producers and consumers. Policies are too often shims and stopgaps to try to mitigate more fundamental problems.

Putting consumers and producers together can do much of the work of regulation for you. When producers can see the impact that their business decisions have on their customers, they instinctively change their behavior to generate more positive effects. They yearn to know more about the people on the other side of the counter. They constantly tweak and modify their methods of production, selling, and engagement to improve their own sales performance. In doing so, they improve the lives of the people they serve.

Looking at what she has accomplished, it can be easy to see Nina as some sort of activist, pushing local food on the populace. And while she does recommend the health benefits of eating local, in-season food, that's not her primary interest. She's there because she's a capitalist. She wants to make money. Nina is an entrepreneur, and a damn good one. She operates all of her markets as for-profit entities, defying those who believe farmers' markets can't make money. The company earns a percentage of farmers' total sales and does quite well in the process. Most supermarkets have gross margins of approximately 25 percent. London Farmers' Markets, commands gross margins in excess of 60 percent. At the end of the day, supermarkets have a net margin of about 6 percent. Nina's company pulls in net margins in the high 20s. Figures like that fly in the face of conventional supermarket wisdom that says you can't make a profit selling raw food. "People say we raised incomes and even saved farms," Nina says. "We just set out to create a market where farmers could sell and eaters could buy."

London Farmers' Markets also confounds the notion that people shop at farmers' markets out of pity for family farmers whose profits have eroded over time. Charity isn't welcome at the markets, and buyers don't deliver it. "The buyers are ruthless," Nina says. She and her managers let their producers live and die by how well their food meets the needs of shoppers. When they offer great food, producers succeed. When they offer poor-quality food, the buyers ignore them and move onto the next stall.

Nina is perfectly willing to let her farmers fail at the market when they fail to meet their customers' needs. She also encourages real competition the likes of which is unheard of in her category. To avoid saturation of any one kind of food, many farmers' markets establish quotas. Only one vendor sells lamb chops, while another sells apples, and so on. Nina recoils at this. "You might as well pretend that you're in the Soviet Union." Instead, she has had new vendors enter her markets and beat out long-standing ones. "Capitalism really works. I respect my farmers, and I respect my buyers. I trust their abilities."

WHEN PRODUCERS MEET CONSUMERS

What Zildjian and the London Farmers' Markets reflect in their way of doing business is important for companies of all sizes to consider. By keeping their customers close to them, these organizations have enjoyed consistent, profitable growth. That's because when producers and consumers meet each other face to face, they form an empathic connection. They see each other as people and treat each other better as a result. Producers move to better methods of production, because they know that their consumers care about the environment and the health of their families. They cut fewer corners and make choices that are ethically right, because they know that the consumers who could be affected by their decisions are real people with feelings and needs of their own.

At the same time, consumers act differently toward producers when they see them not as companies, but as real people.

Whether they're picking up a couple of carrots at the farmers' market, choosing a cymbal for their next performance, or buying an air-conditioning system for the office that they manage, people have a natural tendency to connect with other human beings. That empathic connection then enables a better transaction. Consumers become more loyal and more willing to try new products from the same company. They recommend favorite producers to their friends. They gladly pay premium prices to get products and services that connect with them. People want to make connections with the folks they do business with.

The benefits of making commerce more immediate are incredibly tangible. When producers and consumers see each other as actual people, capitalism in its oldest form reemerges. In that moment, both sides can see the real territory of life instead of the maps that we've created as substitutes. But most companies serve thousands, if not millions, of people. These people live in many countries, have many backgrounds, and are interested in many different products. Managers often need maps just to get around their own organizations, let alone understand all the people they serve. When you grow tomatoes and sell them at the farmers' market, it isn't a challenge to empathize with the folks who buy your tomatoes. The challenge of developing empathy is much greater for large organizations that need to connect with many kinds of people. No company can get to that level of empathy overnight. But any company can get started on that path by adapting to how human beings are biologically wired.

PART II

Creating Widespread Empathy

FOUR

The Power of Affinity

*The quickest way to have empathy for someone
else is to be just like them. For companies,
the answer is to hire their customers.*

WE'VE ALREADY SEEN how Microsoft was able to succeed quickly with Xbox when the company hired hardcore gamers to develop its first console. Those gamers successfully navigated the trade-offs and compromises of the product development process to create an amazing game system that people like them would want to play. But for anyone seeking to create widespread empathy in their own organization, there's more to the story. And it starts with a guy named Seamus.

By the time 26-year-old Seamus Blackley arrived at Microsoft's headquarters to work as a graphics programmer, he was trying to climb out of the depths of professional failure. A tall, imposing figure with an impish grin and a superhero chin, Seamus had once been the toast of the computer game industry for his work on *Flight Unlimited*, an innovative flight simulator. *Unlimited* was the first flying game for PCs that realistically simulated the physics of flight, from lift to drag to thermal currents. The title had been a hit, selling more than 780,000 copies in an industry in which only a handful of games per year ever manage to move even 100,000 units.

The success of *Flight Unlimited* made Seamus the wunder-kind of PC gaming, and he soon accepted a high-profile appointment at Steven Spielberg's DreamWorks Interactive. Working directly with Spielberg, he began developing a game called *Tres-passer* that was based on the tremendously popular *Jurassic Park* movies. From Seamus's perspective, *Trespasser* had the potential to establish video games as an entertainment medium to be taken seriously. Spielberg, David Geffen, and Jeffrey Katzenberg had founded Dreamworks to create the future of entertainment, and Seamus was working to show them that video games could be that future. Collaborating with Spielberg, Seamus had a golden opportunity to demonstrate the creative potential of games to the masses.

Jurassic Park: Trespasser seemed like a sure thing. It brought together a juggernaut entertainment franchise with Steven Spielberg's masterful storytelling and Seamus's envelope-pushing game designs. But when DreamWorks released *Trespasser* for PC, it sold a fraction of the million copies that was expected. Far from changing society's perceptions of video games, *Trespasser* didn't even find an audience among existing gamers. Those who did buy the game found that it performed sluggishly on all but the newest PCs. Despite its ambitious goals, *Trespasser* was a flop.

Devastated, Seamus quit his job at DreamWorks, sure that his career in games was over. He traveled the world, visited his parents for awhile, and finally decided to take what he assumed would be a low-pressure job writing 3-D graphics development tools for Microsoft. Seamus thought he would vanish into the world's biggest software company, make some good money, and let everyone forget all about his meteoric rise and catastrophic fall. Or at least, that was his plan.

In March 1999, Seamus's plan went out the window. Just one month into his employment at Microsoft, Sony announced

PlayStation 2, and the media hype made Seamus kind of mad. He found Sony's system thoroughly unimpressive. Though powerful, the console's complex design made game developers' jobs difficult. It used an entirely new architecture and a wildly different programming philosophy than its predecessor. All the knowledge that game makers had accumulated as they made games for the first PlayStation was now irrelevant. Any experience they had gained from making games for PCs was equally irrelevant. Game developers would basically have to start from scratch to make anything great. What a waste of good processing power, Seamus thought. Someone ought to do something. In that moment, a light went on in his brain. As he later recalled, "I realized we could make a sooperdooper bad-ass gaming console."

Kicking into action, Seamus and co-conspirators Ted Hase, Kevin Bachus, and Otto Berkes put together a proposal for the game system that they would want to play. Their plan was to create programming tools that would be familiar to anyone who had ever designed a game for Windows, but then couple them to hardware that would have gaming capabilities more powerful than most PCs. Part of the success of any game console is its capability to attract third-party developers to create popular new game titles. Seamus and his team planned to make a system that developers would consider a canvas for their creativity. The proposed system would use the same programming tools that developers already used to make games for home PCs. The leap to a console would be easy for anyone who had ever made a game for Windows. The team called their idea Xbox, and the more they thought about it, the more they were sure that they were onto something.

The Xbox project quickly won approval from Microsoft CEO Bill Gates. Gates had earlier tried to convince Sony to use Microsoft software on the PlayStation 2, but the Japanese company had rejected his entreaties. Gates was now eager to show how Microsoft could make a video game system that was better than Sony's. Gates helped expand and fund the project, assembling a larger team of engineers, designers, and marketers and charging them with creating the ultimate game console. J Allard, the man credited with helping Microsoft respond to the threat of the Internet, was named project manager. To win, the members of the team decided that they wouldn't try to be everything to everyone. Instead, they would focus on hardcore gamers who loved to spend late nights and lost weekends playing epic, intense, and sometimes violent games that got their adrenaline flowing—guys like Seamus Blackley. Seamus knew exactly what other guys like him were looking for. Unlike the games from Nintendo and Sony, Xbox would be about immersive, interactive entertainment of the highest order. It would be for gamers and the artists who made games.

As the project picked up steam, Seamus shared his vision with the independent game developers he wanted to empower. He wanted to make it clear that Microsoft was entering the market to help make great games—not to crush existing competition. He found that most of the third-party game studios were sick and tired of being pushed around by Sony and Nintendo, the industry's traditional powers. They were tired of having to relearn how to make games every time a new platform emerged. As they saw it, Xbox needed to be so familiar that they could spend their energy on artistic expression instead of basic functionality. They said that if he could get Microsoft to make a console with a PC processor and a lightning-fast graphics processor, Xbox could give Sony a run for its money.

Bearing these two groups in mind, hardcore gamers and developers, the Xbox team set about the business of building a game that they themselves would want to play. Executives at

Microsoft gave the Xbox team unprecedented room to work differently. Xbox was free from typical corporate restrictions, including an existing Microsoft mandate that all of its hardware must run the Windows operating system. Microsoft was also prepared to spend billions of dollars to beat Sony. That meant that when the console proved more expensive to build than initially anticipated, the team was able to stick to its guns and include a cutting-edge graphics card from NVIDIA as had been promised to the developers. Though there were plenty of plausible arguments and market research reports in favor of cutting a few corners on the Xbox, the team didn't fall for them.

Xbox was launched in the fall of 2001, less than three years after Seamus was hired. It was a hit from day one. Despite enormous industry skepticism, Xbox ate into Sony's enormous lead in the market and became a beloved icon of the gamer set. By paying attention to other people like themselves, the developers of the Xbox entered a mature market and became immediately competitive. In the next generation, Microsoft's Xbox 360 outsold Sony's PlayStation 3 by almost two to one.

BIRDS OF A FEATHER

The simplest way to have empathy for other people is to be just like them. A sense of affinity can deliver clarity to often difficult and complex situations. It obliterates faulty assumptions and sharpens ambiguous data. With that kind of empathic connection, people inside an organization spend a lot less time arguing about what customers think or what the research is showing—they just know what to do.

Empathy for gamers and developers fueled the rise of the Xbox because the people who made the system were a lot like the people who would play it. This highlights something that all

people intuitively understand: It's easy to get along with someone who is like you. In kindergarten, boys tend to hang out with
boys, and girls hang out with girls. In high school, the jocks tend
to hang out with other jocks, while the kids in the band hang
out with other kids in the band. People with common political
leanings demonstrate a similar ability to connect. And it comes
as no surprise that people who enjoy bowling are more likely
to make friends with other bowlers. That's just how our social
interactions work.

Research now suggests that there's a deep-seated biological reason for why we connect more easily with people like
ourselves. Adrianna Jenkins, a psychology graduate student
at Harvard University, created a study in 2007 that tested how
our brains distinguish between people who seem similar to
us and those who are different. In her experiment, volunteers
walked into a research facility, where they read brief descriptions of two college students. Though the details of their lives
were intentionally vague, one of the students was portrayed as
a liberal from New England attending an exclusive private college, and the other was a conservative Midwesterner enrolled
at a large public university. The volunteers were placed into a
functional magnetic resonance imaging chamber, which can
measure blood flow to different parts of the brain to indicate
neural activity. The researchers asked them to say which of the
two characters they identified with more closely. Then, as the
MRI scanned their brains for activity, the volunteers were asked
a series of questions about themselves and about the two characters: What did the liberal person think about being the center
of attention? What about the conservative? What did the study
volunteer think about being at the center of attention?

The researchers repeated this process with many different
questions and a number of different participants. Over time, a

consistent pattern of activity emerged. A set of neurons in participants' brains that were concerned with self-reference and identity became active both when the participants talked about themselves and when they talked about the character they identified with. Interestingly, those parts of the brain did nothing when the volunteers had to think about the character they didn't identify with. This study suggests something fascinating about the human brain: When we think about people that are like ourselves, we have no difficulty imagining how they might react to a given situation because we reflect their way of thinking. It's literally as if we're thinking about ourselves. But when forced to think about people who seem quite different from us, we lack that same intuition. That's why we find it easier to make friends with people like us, to do business with them, and even to create things that they find appealing. We can spend less time arguing about goals and cut to the chase. We can even spot an essential truth that no one else has the common sense to notice.

IT'S THE ECONOMY, STUPID

One day in 1992, James Carville got up from his desk and walked to a wall at the center of the office where he worked. Carville, a brash, argumentative lawyer from the Louisiana swampland, pulled out a marker and scrawled three statements on a white board in big capital letters:

CHANGE VS. MORE OF THE SAME
THE ECONOMY, STUPID
DON'T FORGET HEALTHCARE

As he finished, Carville looked around the room, making sure that everyone working with him on Bill Clinton's presidential campaign took the message to heart. Trapped between incumbent President George Bush and third-party challenger Ross Perot, the Clinton campaign had been struggling to catch up. Carville was known as the Ragin' Cajun for his proclivity to go off on a rant when he had something important to say. And that day, he had discovered the key to the election. Forget what the polls said. Forget what the media was talking about. Forget what the other candidates thought mattered. As far as Carville was concerned, the truth of the 1992 election was this: There's a recession on, ordinary folks are hurting, and this campaign and the government can do something about it. It's the economy, stupid. Fix that, and the world will beat a path to our door.

Like anyone else, Carville had been a product of his environment. And his environment had been every bit as tough, opinionated, and concerned with the economy as he would one day become. James was actually just the most recent in a long line of tough-as-nails Carvilles. He had been born and raised in the southern Louisiana town of Carville, a sweltering, swampy bend in the Mississippi River about a half-hour south of Baton Rouge. The town had been named after his family because the Carvilles had long served as the postmasters for the area. The family took the position very seriously, and they were proud to work for the federal government. James's father, Chester, had worked for the government, too. Chester was a soldier and had been stationed at Georgia's Fort Benning at the tail end of World War II when his wife, Lucille, gave birth to James, their first child. After the war, the couple would bring seven more children into the world, and they raised every single one of them in Carville.

As James grew up, his family worked hard to get by. Chester ran a struggling general store in addition to fulfilling his duties as postmaster. Lucille sold encyclopedias door to door. The Carvilles didn't have much money, but with hard work and a little help from the government, they managed to make ends meet.

James joined the Marines after he graduated from high school, and the G.I. Bill paid for him to go to college and, eventually, law school. Though he grew up in the Louisiana swamp, James went on to become a widely respected political consultant. Sure, he succeeded, in no small part, thanks to his legendary stubbornness, but James recognized that the government's help with his education had made his dreams possible. As he would proclaim in his book *We're Right, They're Wrong*, "You will never catch me saying I'm a self-made man." James had been a direct beneficiary of the power of government to create opportunities for people who otherwise had few prospects for advancement. For him, the promise was real.

That mentality stayed with him as he worked with Clinton on the '92 campaign. Carville recognized that the working class was once again getting crushed under the weight of a slow, cumbersome economy. He saw the pain that gripped the country, and he knew that the government could help through aid for education, tax relief, and healthcare programs for America's working class. Though he knew that Big Government is a bogeyman in the United States, he also knew that decent, hard-working folks like his own parents would welcome the assistance they needed to work toward their dreams. People care about their ability to feed their kids, advance in society, and look themselves in the mirror with pride. Put it on the wall, that's the story: It's the economy, stupid.

James Carville's simple message for the Clinton campaign resonated because it summed up what people all around the country were feeling. Carville's message reflected the outlook of working Americans, and working Americans, in turn, rallied to his message. When people feel understood, they almost always react positively. They reward our empathy by saying, "That guy gets us."

Of course, Carville's message might have been lost without
an effective messenger. Bill Clinton made "It's the economy,
stupid," a household phrase. He transformed Carville's outlook
into a campaign platform. Clinton was able to connect with
working-class Americans as one of their own. Raised in rural
Arkansas first by his grandparents and then by his mother and
an abusive, alcoholic stepfather, Clinton started life with little
money or hope. He was a hard-working Southerner who played
the saxophone, admitted to trying marijuana (didn't inhale),
and looked out for a troubled half-brother who had done time
for drug possession. Humble upbringing, dysfunctional family,
and all, Bill Clinton was one of us.

Clinton took Carville's strategy and ran with it. Over and
over, he broadcast the message that he understood the pain that
the slowing economy was causing. He channeled the distress of
Americans who had lost their jobs and were struggling to make
ends meet. He talked about the economy first, he talked about it
second, and he talked about it third. Clinton made his rhetoric
real by recalling the tough times that he had experienced growing up in Hope, Arkansas. And little by little, this once-obscure
Southern governor began to rise in the polls.

As the economy grew weaker, the American people began
to notice how little their sitting president's life resembled their
own. The son of a U.S. Senator from Massachusetts, George H.W.
Bush had been a Congressman from Texas, a U.N. ambassador,
the chairman of the Republican National Committee, and even
the director of the CIA before he became Ronald Reagan's vice
president. The only nonpolitical work Bush had ever done was
managing a string of oil exploration projects with family friends.
Though he claimed Texas as his home, Bush spoke with a New
England accent. He was a man who had never worried about
where his next meal was coming from, and he had wandered the

corridors of power since he learned to crawl. He understood in an abstract sense that the recession was bad for Americans, but he had no personal connection to that reality.

That became abundantly clear in February 1992, when a PR visit to a grocers' convention turned into a nightmare for the Bush campaign. Touring the trade show's floors, Bush saw demonstrations of many new technologies, including the latest barcode scanners. He was impressed by what he saw—so impressed, in fact, that *The New York Times* reported that Bush said he had never before seen a check-out scanner, even though the technology had first appeared in stores in 1976. Although the report was later proven false, it was enough to make Bush look dangerously out of touch. After all, he had been in political or bureaucratic office nonstop since 1966. It seemed entirely possible that he had never been to the supermarket since then!

His campaign managers tried to defuse the story but made things worse instead. They offered up evidence that the president had, indeed bought his own groceries...once. A year earlier. In the New England resort town of Kennebunkport, Maine, where his family owned not just a cottage, but a nine-bedroom estate with a four-car garage on a private peninsula that jutted into the ocean. By trying to make the president appear more normal, Bush's campaign inadvertently highlighted how little his life resembled that of an ordinary American. The stories for the two candidates were clear: Bush was a product of a lifetime spent in Washington. Clinton was a guy who knew what it meant to be poor and hungry. President Bush had people who did his grocery shopping for him. Clinton knew that it was the economy, stupid.

With considerable help from third-party candidate Ross Perot, a Texas businessman who also spoke to the economic pain of everyday Americans, Clinton managed the improbable. He defeated Bush and claimed the White House. Though the results were close, his victory should never have been possible in the first place against a strong, sitting president. Bush had lost an insurmountable lead, in part because he couldn't connect with ordinary people. On point after point, Clinton excelled by acting like a regular guy, someone you might want to hang out with at the bar after work. Bush seemed like the cranky old neighbor who wouldn't give you your baseball back if you accidentally hit it into his yard.

By reflecting the worldview of average Americans, James Carville's strategy won the election. Clinton's victory was a triumph of empathy over experience. George H. W. Bush spent more time working for the federal government prior to his presidency than almost any other candidate in the history of the office. But none of that mattered when his fellow Americans got inspired by a man who really understood what their lives were like. Ironically, eight years after Clinton was elected president, a second George Bush, the son of the former president, won the nation's highest office partly because he, too, seemed like an ordinary guy. Despite a modest resume and no foreign policy experience to speak of, George W. Bush defeated eminently qualified Vice President Al Gore because the younger Bush seemed more like a normal person. The younger Bush struck people as an easygoing guy, while Gore seemed like the kind of smarty-pants intellectual who would start lecturing you on the minutiae of policy the second you met him. Both elections were decided on the basis of empathy. When candidates reflect the way America likes to see itself, they win at the polls.

THE CHALLENGES OF SUCCESS

In many ways, Bill Clinton's stunning victory in the 1992 presidential election came down to one factor: Clinton could connect with the American people, and the incumbent president couldn't. In many ways, George H.W. Bush was done in by his own achievements. He had been tremendously successful in serving his country, from his days as a naval pilot to his days in the White House. The reason that he fell out of step with the American people is that his life was extraordinary. He solved problems no one else faced. He met people no one else did. He traveled to countries that few Americans ever do. And with each step forward, President Bush grew further and further away from the majority of the American people he was so proud to serve. Bush's challenge was that the only other people like him were other diplomats, politicians, and millionaires. He was a victim of his own success.

Interestingly, Microsoft's Xbox ran into the same problem. Even as Microsoft claimed the hardcore gamer market lead, a flaw in the Xbox strategy became apparent. As it turns out, there really aren't that many hardcore gamers out there. And when Nintendo launched a new system in 2006 called the Wii that focused on casual, fun video games for the whole family, Microsoft was poorly positioned to respond. In just ten months, Wii overtook the Xbox 360's global lead in the console market and overshadowed the launch of Sony's PlayStation 3. The Xbox team's empathy for gamers helped Microsoft to capture the existing gaming market. Nintendo's interest in nongamers helped it to open up a completely new market for casual gaming. Microsoft had become so successful in reflecting the outlook of gamers that it had become blind to everyone else.

That's the problem with success: It can make you lose touch with the world around you. When companies are founded, their leaders often have a strong intuitive sense for their customers. Microsoft was founded in the early 1970s by a couple of geeky computer programmers who wanted to serve other geeky computer programmers. Nike was founded by a track coach and a few of his best runners who wanted to make great running shoes. In those early days, neither company had particularly excellent operations, but that didn't matter, because they were making stuff for other people like them. Microsoft made great programming tools because it was made up of programmers. Nike made great shoes because it was made up of runners.

But as companies grow larger and more prosperous, they start to look less and less like their customers. Airline executives stop flying economy class. The little tomato sauce company starts to attract Harvard MBAs who eat out all the time and never cook their own spaghetti. The lives of the people that the company employs become less and less like the lives of ordinary folks. Continued for too long, this gap can grow into an overwhelming gulf between the people inside of a company and everyone else.

LIFE ON THE A PLAN

Although the automobile was first invented in Europe, it was the men and women of Detroit, Michigan who made the car a fixture of our everyday lives. From the first factory that Ransom E. Olds opened in Lansing to Henry Ford's legendary production lines in Dearborn, Michigan, was a place built by and for the car. And its economy reflected that. Well into the late 1970s, the Detroit area was one of the wealthiest parts of the country. For generations, people in cities like Lansing, Flint, and Auburn Hills were virtually guaranteed good jobs at great wages down at the local auto factory the day they graduated from high school. The entire region of southeastern Michigan shaped itself to reflect the source of its prosperity. Michigan developed the biggest freeways, the broadest avenues, and the most conspicuous cruising routes in the country. Ford, General Motors, and Chrysler were strong, and they lifted everyone else up along with them.

In recent years, however, American car makers have found themselves struggling to survive. Japanese, German, and Korean competitors have decimated the Big Three's market share. Where Cadillac and Lincoln once dominated the market for luxury cars, Lexus now stands as the industry leader. An over-reliance on SUVs and large trucks left American manufacturers unprepared to respond to skyrocketing oil prices. Automakers have found themselves saddled with ballooning healthcare costs and financial commitments to retirees who are living a lot longer than previous generations. What's most troubling is that Ford, GM, and Chrysler seem unable to make cars that people want to buy. Sales in recent years have largely come in the wake of steep rebates that temporarily increased market share but killed profitability. Depending on the brand, nearly a third of sales volume comes from fleet sales to rental car companies, which purchase their vehicles at a heavy discount.

While this situation is dire, it didn't happen overnight. For the Big Three, the last several decades have looked like a car wreck in slow motion. In 1984, domestic manufacturers commanded 81% of the U.S. car market. Today, they own less than 50%. Declines in sales were gradual, interrupted only by a temporary boost from truck and SUV sales in the 1990s.

Yet, throughout that time, U.S. auto executives behaved as if foreign competition was a temporary blip that would go away. They resisted increases in fuel efficiency standards even as German and Japanese manufacturers invested in diesel and hybrid electric technology. They put off major investments that would increase product quality. And they were slow to adapt to customer preferences in vehicle type, features, and styling. How

did they let this happen? It wasn't through a lack of intelligence.
American automakers have always been able to attract some of
the nation's best talent. The cause might have been a systemic
lack of empathy.

As we've seen, success can create its own challenges. During their heyday, U.S. automakers created programs that gave
their top managers use of their latest vehicles for next to nothing. Senior executives didn't even have to pump their own gas.
At the same time, auto companies created the A Plan, which
offered every employee a deep discount any time they decided
to buy a new car. Those discounts applied to friends and family
of employees, too. Anyone connected to a car company could
buy a brand-new American car at prices below wholesale. While
this made it great to be a car company employee, it also served
to make people at car companies different from the rest of us.
Drivers in Detroit switch cars more often and for less money
than people anywhere else in the country. And this has had
unexpected consequences for the region.

Driving around Detroit, it's easy to see the problem. The
roads of southeastern Michigan look nothing like the rest of
the country. While American manufacturers command an ever
smaller share of the domestic car market, Detroit's highways
continue to be filled with mostly American cars. Hondas and
Toyotas are still a relatively rare sight. The Toyota Camry is
the number one passenger car in America, but it takes a while
to find one on the streets of Detroit. Instead, rush hour traffic
is a display of vehicles that other Americans rarely see. Many
people drive models that were never popular with anyone
who couldn't get a discount. Though originally intended as an
employee incentive, the A Plan has had the unintended conse-
quence of making Detroit a place that no longer resembles the
rest of the country. In that kind of environment, it's difficult

for employees of Ford, GM, and Chrysler to truly reflect their customers.

To make matters worse, Ford announced in 2006 that the parking lot at its Dearborn Truck Plant would be open only to employees who drove vehicles built by Ford or one of its subsidiaries. Given Ford's dire situation at the time, a demand for solidarity from its employees must have felt like the right thing to do. In actuality, it further separated the company from the rest of the country and distorted how its employees saw the world. After all, how can you beat your competitors if you never really see what they offer? This was one example of when it might have been better for Ford to keep its enemies closer.

I have family in Detroit, so this issue is rather personal for me. By making the region an edifice to itself, U.S. automakers cut themselves off from the rest of the country. Then, devoid of any real empathy for ordinary customers, decision makers made poor choices. They lived in a bubble. Southeastern Michigan is filled with good people who worked hard for decades and brought a lot of benefit to the rest of the country. But their leaders let them down.

The challenges that face leaders of industry and government in Detroit are complex and difficult to resolve. The region is wracked with high unemployment, mounting debt, and a struggling cornerstone industry. But this much is certain: Those problems will never be fixed unless Detroit's leaders learn to see the world the way everyone else does.

CHOOSING NOT TO REFLECT

The differences between the people inside a company and the people they serve don't have to be dramatic to cause significant problems. Sometimes, the most basic distinctions can lead to the greatest trouble. Many of Detroit's problems stem from the fact that decision makers have little incentive to try out other manufacturers' cars. They don't view the market through the eyes of ordinary Americans.

Of course, not every company is a business that lends itself to being a direct reflection of its customers. It's relatively easy for an office chair manufacturer to know what its customers are going through. It's harder for a pharmaceutical company to do the same. It's nonetheless unfortunate to see the number of companies that have the opportunity to reflect what they see and choose not to.

I see it all the time in my work for Jump. Companies that are trying to figure out how to open new markets, create success-ful new products, or launch entirely new businesses often invite me to meet with their leaders. Several years ago, I was called in to chat with the senior leadership of Jell-O, the brand that made instant gelatin a staple of American picnics and potlucks. Jell-O was starting to struggle. The brand's sales were slipping, and revenues from new products weren't making up for the loss. Something needed to change.

The gathered team was uncertain about how to fix the chal-lenges it faced. People were eating less Jell-O, and the company couldn't understand why that was happening. For several hours, we sat through presentation after presentation of depressing quantitative research that described the situation. At some point, I had to raise my hand. I looked around the room and asked if anyone there had eaten any Jell-O in the past six months. No one raised a hand. Interesting, I said. Maybe that was part of the problem. While Detroit was too focused on its own products, the Jell-O team seemed disconnected from theirs. Either way, both groups seemed deliberately out of touch with the rest of the world.

FIVE

Walking in Someone Else's Shoes

*It's often not possible or not enough to hire
your customers. To continue to grow and
prosper, you have to step outside of yourself
and walk in someone else's shoes.*

HIRING YOUR CUSTOMERS is one of the quickest ways to start realizing the benefits of empathy. But as we've seen, that alone can be quite limiting. Having a deep connection to one type of person can actually hinder you from connecting with other types of people or make you insensitive to changes in the market. For companies that cater to a variety of people, simply reflecting a single point of view isn't enough. For them, the ability to empathize with multiple types of people can be the difference between success and failure. Companies need the curiosity and talent to connect with the many different kinds of people they serve. They need to step outside of themselves and see how different the world can look through someone else's eyes.

One of the big assignments in my Needfinding class at Stanford is called the Moccasins project. It's a reference to the Native American exhortation to not judge another man before you've walked a mile in his moccasins. We ask students to spend time with a person who's completely different from themselves and then try to walk in their shoes. Over the years, students have worked as car salesmen, picked grapes with migrant workers, tried to pass themselves off as people of the opposite sex, and even learned how to be lion tamers. The exercise is a chance for students to experience the kind of reframe that happened to Pattie Moore when she stepped into the world of the elderly. The project was a part of the class long before I ever started teaching it. In fact, the reason I'm so passionate about teaching the class has a lot to do with my own experience doing the Moccasins project when I was a student.

When I got the assignment, I thought of my friend Muffy Davis. Muffy lived in my dorm and was an Olympic-level skier who had spent most of her life in the snowbound paradise of Sun Valley, Idaho. Tragically, Muffy had slammed into a tree while on a training run, and the accident had left her paralyzed from the waist down. After the accident, she came to spend most of her waking hours in a wheelchair. Muffy is an amazing woman who embodies the kind of strength and determination that most of us can only aspire to. When I met her, I couldn't imagine what she had to go through on a daily basis. The assignment offered me a chance to get a glimpse.

It quickly became clear to me that the exercise needed to be a full-time immersion. Unlike being a car salesman or a lion tamer, the disabled can't pack up and leave their disability behind at the end of a long day. To really understand what life was like for Muffy, I needed to be in a wheelchair nonstop, from the time I lifted myself out of bed in the morning until the time I pulled myself back into bed at night. I needed to bind my legs together so I couldn't walk at all. Fortunately, our dorm was equipped with a handicapped-accessible toilet and shower on the ground floor, so I switched rooms with a friend to be closer to those facilities.

The first day in the chair was, without a doubt, the most frustrating. I found a store that rented wheelchairs in downtown Palo Alto. They had told me over the phone that I could rent a wheelchair for forty dollars a month. Fifty dollars would get me an extra-lightweight model. As I headed over to the store, I envisioned a chair like Muffy's. Her chair was a sexy black model that looked like it could keep up in the Tour de France. I walked into the store and showed the sales clerk the chair that I wanted. "No, no, sir," I was told. "That wheelchair isn't for rent. I'll have our man bring out the lightweight rental model." He returned shortly pushing a chair that fell far short of my expectations. To my dismay, it was made of heavy, tubular steel, with a sticky Naugahyde seat. It looked like a chair for a hospital patient. I didn't want to get into it, because I didn't want people to think that there was something wrong with me.

Muffy laughed when she saw my chair for the first time. "Good luck," she said, "You're going to totally die in that thing." Then she reminded me that everyone who gets a wheelchair has to use this kind until a custom chair can be built for them. And that's if you're lucky. Most people can't afford the several thousand dollars that a better chair will run you.

My first task in the chair was to get to class. Rolling across campus seemed like an unending journey, compounded by the rain and mud that's an inevitable part of February in Northern California. My glasses steamed up so that I couldn't see. Water began to pool in the seat, and I was soaked to the skin. Later on, when I asked Muffy what I was supposed to do when it rained, her answer was simple. "You get wet."

Twice along the way to class, my hands slipped on the wheels and fell into the brake mechanisms. Each time, the sharp edge on the mechanism would cut the top of my thumbs. This painful experience would occur eight or ten times a day, causing small repeat-puncture wounds on both hands. I continuously cursed the mechanical designers who never bothered to get in their own chair and go for a roll. Had they done so, a few quick scars would have shown them that they needed to rethink the brakes.

I finally arrived at class five minutes late. Rolling into the auditorium, I struggled to keep the chair from sliding down the steep aisle. The last thing I needed was to crash into the front wall. A friend of mine grabbed the daily handouts for me since they were on the aisle floor out of reach. With no place to keep the papers, I put them in my mouth as I slid down to the front of the class. Soaking wet and shivering, I tried to focus on the lecture.

My mouth came in handy again at lunch, and not just for eating. Unable to get home in time to eat and get back for class, I decided to grab some pizza in the student union. Despite the lunchtime crowd, I found people were nice enough to me. Everyone who saw me coming gave me more than enough room to get past them. My only obstacles were the backpacks and purses that lay in the aisles. Ordering was fairly easy, although the high glass counter was a bit intimidating and made me feel like I was three years old. The soda fountain was too high for me to activate and still see inside the cup. I had to stop filling the cup every few seconds to check and see how far it had filled. Once filled, the cup presented another problem. I could put my pizza on my lap, but where would I put my cup as I tried to find a seat? With no other option, I put the brim of the cup in my mouth and bit down as hard as I could. As I searched through the crowd for a place to sit, I was careful not to drop my liquid feedbag. I wondered if this comical scene only added to the perception that there was something wrong with me.

I also discovered that riding in a wheelchair is not the cleanest of experiences. Any dirt on the road rides up onto the wheels and eventually rubs onto your hands. Wet mud is gross, and dry roads leave black soot on your palms that has to be washed off about five times a day. It's a little like walking on your hands. Between the dirty hands and the mouth-holding thing, I was ashamed to admit that I felt a little like a cocker spaniel. Moreover, it took me twice as long to get to classes as it did when I walked. Things got so bad that I was forced to decide which classes to skip on any given day. I simply had to do less.

Within a few days, I had gotten used to some of the physical challenges of being in a wheelchair. Only then did I start to notice the loneliness. When you sit in a wheelchair, you're a lot shorter than everyone else. People start talking over your head, and you struggle to be a part of the conversation. I noticed that I responded to the exclusion by getting quieter.

My frustration had started to be replaced by a melancholy resignation. When the weekend came, I was invited to a party on the other side of campus. At the last minute, I changed my mind and decided to stay home. I told myself that it was late and I was catching a cold. Deep down, I knew that I just didn't want to deal with the hassle of being in the wheelchair. Things got worse. The next day, I stayed in bed for most of the day. I again rationalized that I was getting sick and needed the extra rest. In truth, I'd wake up, look over at the wheelchair, and then go back to sleep. It was easier to stay in bed than deal with life. The next day, I stopped going to class altogether.

I was clearly experiencing a depression that was either caused or exacerbated by my physical condition. I had planned on spending only three days in the chair. But as the week ended, I realized that I couldn't leave yet. All that I had experienced was misery and pain. And that wasn't news. No one stays in a wheelchair by choice. They learn to live with it. I needed to find out what life was like on the other side of depression. I couldn't end the exercise until I could see what that was like. I needed to get back in the chair and get out of my room.

Within another day or two, life started to feel normal again. I even started to forget that I was in a wheelchair. When a friend that I hadn't seen in a while asked what had happened to me, it took me a second to realize that he was asking about the chair. It had become normal for me. I was finally able to get beyond my own emotional response to the wheelchair, and I started to look at the world around me. I began to study other people. On the whole, I found that other people went out of their way to be nice to me, opening doors for me or waiting for me to catch up— they seemed to feel a need to act politely toward me. Indeed, I wondered if I ever got treated so nicely on two feet. When I thanked the guy at the movie theater for the hot dog that he'd just handed me, he responded, "Thank you sir, I'm glad I could help you." Usually, all I got was a grunt. Despite all this, there seemed to be a touch of sadness in people's interactions with me. I felt that I was spoken to in the same mild-mannered fashion that we tend to speak to hospital patients and anyone else who shouldn't be disturbed. One friend admitted that I somehow looked "sadder" in a wheelchair and that it really bummed him out to see me like that. His uneasy politeness couldn't be helped. If I had been in his shoes, I would probably have acted the same way.

Throughout my time in the chair, the only people who seemed insensitive were the ones who had designed the physical objects that acted as barriers in my life. I once tried to use the bathroom adjoining my dorm's computer cluster. Luckily, it was large enough for me to squeeze inside with my chair. My happiness was stopped short when, after closing the door, I looked for the paper toilet liners, only to see them in a receptacle mounted on the wall, three and a half feet over my head. Embarrassed, I had to ask a friend to get one down for me. When I complained about the container's placement, she reminded me that this bathroom wasn't "designed for the disabled," as if placing the liners two feet lower would have somehow hurt the feelings of tall, walking people. I was perplexed. Shouldn't a bathroom that excluded use by the disabled, the elderly, children, and short people instead be deemed "designed for no one?"

After staying in a wheelchair for two weeks, I thought I was ready to stand up and walk again. But when the time came, I found that I couldn't. This time, it was because of my friend, Muffy. The Olympics in Albertville, France, had just begun, and the skiing events were being televised. This was the first Winter Olympics since Muffy had her accident. She had to watch from her wheelchair as the women who should have been her teammates sliced gracefully down the slopes. It seemed like a particularly hard time for her, and a difficult time for me to walk away. Now that I had tried to enter her life, it seemed like there was no way to make a graceful exit—no way of saying, "Well, thanks for the experience, I'll be going back to walking now." Rather than face that conversation, I decided to stay in the chair for a few more days. In fact, I might have stayed in the wheelchair for the rest of the school year if Muffy hadn't intervened. Sensing what I was going through, she pulled me aside and told me that it was time to get out.

Knowing what I know now, I don't think I would do it again. Not because it was too physically or emotionally challenging, but because I had tried to enter the life of someone I already knew. And the psychological cost on both of us probably wasn't worth it. Now, when I teach the class, I forbid students from walking in the shoes of anyone they already know. Ironically, a little bit of distance makes it easier to get closer.

In the time I spent in a wheelchair, I learned both a tremendous amount and nearly nothing at all. That is to say, while I had a tiny peephole into a very different perspective on life, that perspective was limited by the fact that it was temporary. On some level, I knew I could walk, and that I would be walking again soon. To forget that fact would be to cross over from empathy to arrogance. I am reminded of the book *The Body Silent*, in which anthropologist Robert Murphy recounts his own battle with a spinal tumor and his consequent seven-year confinement to a wheelchair as he progressively lost control of his body. Next to him, I was but a brief visitor with a shallow orientation. Yet even Murphy's experiences don't encompass life in a wheelchair. When asked to comment on Murphy's book, Robert Krauss, another anthropologist and a life-long paraplegic, said that he refused to read the writings of the "Nouveau Crippled."

Walking in someone else's shoes is a powerful way to see the world through someone else's eyes. Not every student who takes my class chooses to engage with another person's condition on the level I did. Hopefully, though, most of them walk away with an experience that shifts how they see the world. They get the opportunity to learn what life is like for someone else. For many, it can be a profound experience. Yet, for all its power, a moccasins exercise isn't the only way to feel what others feel. It turns out that the ability to cast ourselves into the experiences of others doesn't require massive changes in behavior. We do it all the time in small ways, whether we notice it or not. Deep within the human brain lies the ability to look at what other people are going through and map their situation back to our own. Leveraging that ability is simply a matter of unlocking a power that all of us already possess.

MIRROR NEURONS

The human nervous system is one of the most complex structures in our bodies. Many of its mysteries have yet to be fully understood. One thing neuroscientists are reasonably sure of, however, is that whenever we make a conscious action, a specific set of nerve cells called motor neurons light up. These special neurons have an intimate relationship with the muscles that we consciously control—not our heart or our lungs, but the muscles that we associate with action, such as our biceps, triceps, and hamstrings. So, for example, if you turn this page in the book, motor neurons receive the message from your brain that you want to move your right hand toward the corner of the page, grasp the paper and pull gently to the left. While you turn the page, the motor neurons transmit this message to the muscle cells that do the heavy lifting.

What motor neurons can't do is actually make the decision to turn the page in the first place. Before we can motor, something needs to send the signal that we want to do something. And that begins in our brains, far from the muscles that motor neurons are connected to. In the front of the brain is a region called the premotor cortex. It's the area where thinking that precedes action takes place. If you have the thought that you might like to turn a page in this book, the neurons in your premotor cortex become active and prepare to send the signal to the motor neurons. The human nervous center is so sophisticated and optimized for action that this happens nearly instantaneously. It doesn't take a few seconds for you to reach for the page. Thought and action are so inseparable that a rote activity can often feel like a genuinely thoughtless act. But it's not. We have to think about doing something before we can do it. The premotor cortex is one of the most important parts of the human brain. It adds a level of consideration and intention to our actions that allows us to think through the meaning and impacts of our decisions before we take action.

In the mid-1990s, a team of neuroscientists in Italy wanted to better understand how our brains work when we take action. To that end, Giacomo Rizzolatti, Vittorio Gallese, Luciano Fadiga, and Leonardo Fogassi set up a laboratory to study the brains of macaque monkeys. Like most primates, macaques have brains that are similar to ours, only smaller. The scientists ran wires into the premotor cortices of the macaques in the study so that whenever the monkeys picked up an object, a computer would record their brains' activity. When a monkey reached for a banana, a certain group of neurons lit up. When the monkey reached for a block, a different set lit up. When he reached for a peanut, an entirely different group of neurons lit up.

One day, one of the neuroscientists, Fogassi, walked into the lab and picked up a peanut. One of the monkeys watched Fogassi intently. And in that moment when Fogassi picked up the peanut, the neurons in the monkey's brain lit up in the same way they had when the monkey had picked up the peanut himself. Logically, this made no sense at all. Fogassi had picked up the peanut, so only his premotor cortex should have lit up, not the monkey's. But as he watched Fogassi, the monkey's brain reacted as if he were picking up the peanut, too. Intrigued but perplexed, Fogassi and his colleagues ran the experiment several times. They picked up other objects as the monkeys watched, and in each case, the monkeys' brains reacted as though they were performing the actions themselves. This was new. Something in the monkeys' brains was equating the actions of others with their own.

The neuroscientists called their discovery "mirror neurons" because they allow us to replicate in our heads what we see other people doing. Remarkably, mirror neurons not only light up when we perform an action, but also when we watch someone else perform an action. If you turn a page in a book, a specific set of mirror neurons lights up. If you watch someone else turn a page, the same set of mirror neurons lights up. And that's not all. Incredibly, even if someone just describes page-turning to you, a similar set of mirror neurons will light up. As the Italian neuroscientists continued their research, they discovered that everything we do, see others do, or hear described to us is ultimately governed by and filtered through our mirror neurons. This makes mirror neurons incredibly important for learning. When you watch someone else expertly dribble a basketball, your mirror neurons start to help you learn how to get better at it yourself. On a subconscious level, we learn just by watching.

The most incredible power of mirror neurons, however, is their ability to pick up on tacit information about other people. They do more than help you learn; they help you experience other people's lives. Mirror neurons are the reason that when you watch a gory movie, you wince at any acts of violence—your brain reacts as though you're getting attacked. Our brains ultimately experience other people's actions and feelings in the same way that we experience our own. If someone yawns around us, we become more likely to yawn because our mirror neurons put us in the shoes of the yawner. If someone trips and falls down, we rush to their aid because we feel how much it must hurt to fall down. It even works for less concrete actions. If you look across the room and see someone with a disgusted look on their face, you can feel disgusted yourself. If someone is smiling and laughing, you're more likely to smile and laugh. And if someone else is suffering, you will, too.

LAWRENCE TAYLOR BREAKS JOE THEISMANN'S LEG

Lawrence Taylor is the most feared linebacker ever to play professional football. During his thirteen years with the New York Giants, LT would rove from sideline to sideline waiting to pounce on and crush opposing quarterbacks. He would blow them up. LT was more than an intimidating opponent—he was a force of nature. While playing for the Giants, LT set multiple records for quarterback sacks in a season, as well as in a career. He was even named the league's Most Valuable Player in 1986, a rare honor for a defensive player. As the unofficial leader of the Giants' fearsome defense, LT helped the team win two Super Bowl championships.

LT was every bit as ferocious off the field. He once said that the skill that set him apart from other outside linebackers was his ability to drink. He openly admitted to using cocaine. He even claimed that his efforts to undermine his opponents began off the field by sending prostitutes to visit the hotel rooms of opposing quarterbacks the night before an important game. Referees had to keep a constant eye on LT on the field because it was widely assumed that he tried to sneak in illegal hits to wear down other players. It didn't matter who you were, what you were like off the field, or whether you had a family. If you were on the other team, he would eat you up for breakfast. He was a monster.

Even though he was a monster on the field, Lawrence Taylor was still a human being. And that showed through during one moment of incredible violence. On November 18, 1985, LT's Giants were playing their division rivals, the hated Washington Redskins. Everything was going well. LT covered receivers. He pushed his way through the offensive line on every snap. He was unstoppable. But LT wanted more. He was going to make a permanent impression on the Redskins and the viewing audience.

He was going to take down Joe Theismann, the Redskin's MVP quarterback. He just needed his chance.

That moment arrived in the second quarter, when LT expertly read a trick play by the Redskins offense, dashing past blockers toward Theismann, who was looking downfield for a throw. Ducking past one last blocker, LT left his feet and slammed his considerable weight into Theismann's frame from behind, smashing his opponent to the ground. The impact of the hit was considerable—and sickening. Theismann's right leg bent at an unnatural angle as he fell. It was the kind of hit that people don't get up from. LT had gotten exactly what he had wanted the entire game: to take Theismann down.

As soon as he took Theismann down, LT was back up on his feet. Normally, LT would kneel over the head of a fallen quarterback and aggressively point his fingers in his opponent's face. This time, he jumped up and down, motioning furiously toward the Redskins sideline to send help for Theismann. As the Redskins medical crew raced onto the field, LT turned his gaze away from the sideline to look at Theismann's broken body. Horrified by what he saw, he grabbed his helmet's facemask in anguish. As if in a daze, he began to wander in circles. Over and over again, the normally ruthless player checked in on Theismann. LT stayed near his fallen opponent until the medical team carted the quarterback off the field. LT was as engaged in checking on Theismann as members of the Redskins team were. After the game, x-rays revealed that Theismann's right leg had been shattered into a dozen different pieces. He would never play again. LT's hit on Theismann was precisely the sort of impact he had been trained to deliver, and it shifted the game's momentum. But after seeing Theismann, LT was too upset to celebrate. He was shaken.

What Lawrence Taylor felt was more than sympathy or guilt. It was, instead, as if he had been on the receiving end of his own hit. His mirror neurons bombarded him with physical, emotional, and cognitive information about Theismann. Every time he looked at Theismann's mangled leg, he shuddered as if his own leg had been broken. LT intuitively knew what was running through Theismann's head. The quarterback knew, without consulting a doctor, that this would be the injury that ended his career. He had been All-Pro Joe Theismann when he took that snap; now, he was just some guy who had lost his job and might never be able to walk normally again. When something snapped in Theismann's leg, something else snapped in LT's mind. Lawrence Taylor didn't get injured when he sacked Joe Theismann, but he was a firsthand witness to his opponent's agony. Recalling the hit, LT's teammate Carl Banks described the linebacker's reaction: "Lawrence, the guy who made the hit, probably felt worse than Joe at the time."

Mirror neurons don't discriminate. Whether you watch someone else experience something or whether you go through it yourself, mirror neurons collect reams of data that help us make sense of that experience. Lawrence Taylor broke Theismann's leg, but LT's brain responded as if he had attacked himself. That neurological fact might help to explain why, when asked about the hit more than 15 years later, LT claimed he had never watched a replay of the event. Watching the tape would require him to relive his own trauma. Though he stood and Theismann fell, Lawrence Taylor unexpectedly found himself walking in his opponent's shoes. What a painful place to be.

USING YOUR MIRROR NEURONS ON THE JOB

Of all of the many purposes they serve, mirror neurons' ability to gather implicit information about the thoughts, feelings, and senses of other people is perhaps the most fascinating. Mirror neurons are a critical reason that people know how to relate to each other. They help us become friends and act more appropriately. Moreover, mirror neurons help us to put ourselves in someone else's shoes and imagine how they might feel in a given situation. That's why Gina Beebe, an executive at American Girl, could happily tell me that, in a way, she was an eight-year-old girl. Mirror neurons provide a window into the lives of other people.

However, your mirror neurons do have one important limitation: They need firsthand sensory input. They still require you to meet another person to understand what he or she is going through. And that's something many companies don't leave time for: the opportunity for employees to step outside and feel what other people are feeling, think what they're thinking, and see what they're seeing. Companies are made up of people who have mirror neurons. But too many folks working today are operating with mirror neurons that are cut off from the information they need. That's a big problem. After all, how can you understand what it's like to be someone else if you've never even met them?

RUNNING IN THEIR SHOES

Dave Schenone looked in horror at the streak of black ink running down his pant leg. This was bad, because he was on his way to the most important job interview of his life. Dave had never been to Beaverton, Oregon, so he had been following detailed driving directions from the Portland airport. As he passed each landmark on the route, Dave had pulled a marker from between his clenched teeth to quickly check off each milestone on the page. And now, as he rounded the last corner of his journey, he had seen something so wonderful, so flat-out stupefying that his jaw had literally fallen open.

There, in all its glory, stood Nike headquarters. From the day that Dave became a runner, he had identified closely with the Nike brand. Even at sixteen, the company's emotional story had spoken to his athletic aspirations. He knew well that Nike had been founded by University of Oregon track coach Bill Bowerman and runner Phil Knight. Dave knew that Bowerman's Oregon Ducks had gone undefeated for ten straight seasons and had won four NCAA titles. Nike represented running domination, and that's what Dave, a passionate distance runner from the San Francisco Bay Area, wanted to reflect. Seeking to summon the heroes associated with the brand, Dave decided early on that he would always race in Nike gear—Nike shoes, Nike shorts, and Nike jerseys. At races, he would wait until the last possible moment before pulling off his hooded sweatshirt to reveal a jersey emblazoned with Nike's giant swoosh logo. In Dave's mind, Nike made him look like a superhero. And it also made him feel faster.

Dave had been working as an industrial designer for Tandem Computers. Though he worked in high technology, his passion had remained running, and he could often be seen dashing through the hills above Silicon Valley clad head-to-toe in Nike gear. When Nike came calling in 1992, he quickly found himself on a plane bound for Portland.

Driving up to the headquarters, Dave caught a glimpse of the low, grassy berm that encircled the vast campus. More importantly, he had seen other people like him. Runners, lots of them. As they ran by, he realized that Nike must actively encourage people to get out of the office and go for a run during working hours. "I must have lost it," Dave would recall years later. "It was like I had died and gone to heaven." His euphoria in the moment, however, was short-lived. When he finally stopped looking at the runners, he caught sight of the line of ink running down his pant leg. *Oh, great*, he thought. *I've blown it already.*

Mercifully, Dave's interviewers didn't say a word about the ink stain. Chief Marketing Officer Mark Parker, Design Director Tinker Hatfield, and Innovation Director Sandy Bodegger began with the most important question: "Okay, you're from a computer company," Parker said. "Why do you want to be here?" Inhaling sharply, Dave began to explain as succinctly as he could. Two hours after the question was asked, Dave finished answering, though he had needed to leave out a few key points of his philosophy on sports and running for the sake of brevity. Clearly intrigued by Dave's ideas, the trio of interviewers leaned in closer and started to ask his opinions of the company's current portfolio of shoes and gear. As Dave made his way through just his most immediate, top-of-mind thoughts, several more hours went by. Before he really got done with his second question, the sun had already set. It was time for Dave's interviewers to go home. Disappointed that they had never gotten to their third question, they asked if Dave wouldn't mind coming back the next day.

As the group reconvened the next day, Parker began to test the boundaries of Dave's imagination. How did he see the future of sports? Did he have any cool product ideas? How would he lead product innovation for Nike? The duo sat down in a design studio and began to critique recent product concepts, crossing out details and sketching in new ones. Dave dramatically revamped one shoe design in ten minutes. Parker turned his head to one side to look more closely at the sketch and said, "Okay, let's make this thing," approving it for production instantly. Used to the months-long development process common in the computer industry, Dave nodded in stunned silence. After a pause, Parker continued an earlier thought that he hadn't fully articulated. "Dave, I want you to come and do this." He accepted the offer without hesitation. Ink on his slacks or not, Dave was going to work for Nike. He felt faster already.

As a story of empathy, you can't get better than Dave Schenone. Dave is a great reflection of the runners that he designs for. In the years since his job interview, Dave has designed a lot of shoes for Nike and done a whole lot of running on its campus. From the day he started working there, he has expressed his passion for sports and helped Nike translate that passion into tangible business growth. The job has turned out to be a match made in heaven. Based on his background, it would seem safe to assume that Dave's success at Nike stems from his experience as a runner. After all, he's ranked in the top ten in the world for his age group for the Ironman Triathlon. And yes, he can take a quick run in a new pair of shoes and instantly know whether it performs well enough to take to market. But as handy as his own experience can be, Dave says his gut instincts as an athlete can actually get in the way of his work. From his perspective, it doesn't really matter what he thinks about sports. What counts is what *other* people think about sports.

Dave's real job is to understand how the rest of the world thinks and feels about sports. He isn't there to stroke his own ego; he's there to run in other people's shoes. Dave has succeeded at Nike not because he's a great runner, but because he's so fascinated by other people. He cares more than anything about the next generation of runners, and that means putting his own concerns on hold so that he can understand where other people are coming from. Although he graduated from high school in the early 1970s, Dave spends most of his time trying to see the world through the eyes of a teenager.

"You can make product for yourself for a short period of time, but that's easy!" he says. "I know exactly what I would want, and I would just do it. Simple. I get up in the morning excited to go to work because I've got to solve these problems for these kids. The real joy, fascination, intrigue, and excitement for me comes from talking to kids about sports and watching their eyes just kind of glow."

Dave gets goose bumps when he hears high school athletes talk about their training routines and racing rituals. He learns a lot from their stories of victory and defeat. In pursuit of challenges to his instincts and assumptions, Dave spends a lot of time with high school athletes across the country. He visits track meets, gym classes, and cross-country races. He also shops where teenagers shop and hangs out in the neighborhoods where they like to hang out. He even regularly goes running with his sons, both of whom love the feel of a marathon as much as their father does. He does all of these things because he knows that unless Nike understands what a 16-year-old hot shot is really looking for in his or her athletic gear, the company's business will suffer in the long term.

Dave runs in the footsteps of young athletes so that he can think and feel the same way they do. His experience of other people constantly feeds his mirror neurons with explicit and implicit information about the attitudes and mindsets of the teenagers he studies. By developing his own ability to walk in their shoes, Dave has become good at meeting the needs that teenagers have around sports. Over time, his passion has even helped Nike to see that it doesn't just make shoes; it makes the gear that inspires the athlete in all of us. And that can come in the form of watches, sunglasses, heart-rate monitors, and even MP3 players. Since his arrival at Nike in 1992, Dave has helped the company enter several new categories and businesses that it would not have otherwise considered.

At the same time, Dave's passion for running pushes him to continually learn more about what sports means to other people. It's quite likely, in fact, that Dave simply wouldn't be as curious about other people if he weren't working for Nike. His passion went to waste in the computer industry, and that's not coincidental. He wasn't intensely curious about computer users. Dave has a close friend who works in the upper echelons of Starbucks and has occasionally suggested that Dave contemplate moving to Seattle to join the company. Dave hasn't thought about it for a moment. "Starbucks?" he asks. "I don't even like coffee!"

IT STARTS WITH CURIOSITY

The way that Dave Schenone approaches creating new products and developing new markets at Nike exemplifies what Dale Carnegie wrote in *How to Win Friends and Influence People* way back in 1936: "If you want people to be interested in you, take a genuine interest in other people." When you're curious about other people, and want to understand what their lives are like and what they value, you'll inevitably find that you have a better idea of how to connect with them. Dave Schenone isn't a high school athlete anymore, but he shares in their joys and struggles.

We all find it easier to connect with other people who are like us, but that doesn't mean that we can't understand people who are different from us. Thanks to the power of our mirror neurons, any of us has the ability to appreciate and understand people around us. We just need to be curious about them. It's not possible to be all things to all people, but it is possible to be interested in all people. When we do that, we discover that we become more interesting to them, too. The same is true for organizations. If companies want to attract the interest of the outside world, they need to forget about their own problems and start caring about the people they serve.

SIX

Empathy That Lasts

*Bringing people face to face triggers a
caring response. The emotionally charged
memories of that experience can be a
guiding light to stay true to the vision.*

SEVERAL YEARS AGO, a group of senior executives from
Mercedes-Benz wanted to understand how they could make
cars that appealed to young Americans. They were concerned
that Mercedes had become so closely associated with wealthy
Baby Boomers that the brand might have trouble connecting
with a new generation of drivers. They felt the need to reinvent
themselves. They needed to innovate. With that goal in mind,
a group of twenty executives set out on a trip to San Francisco
to meet with experts on innovation. As part of that trip, they
invited a team from Jump to join them for an afternoon.

The meetings were held at the Fairmont, a luxurious hotel in
San Francisco. As the team settled into their chairs, I ran them
through a quick slide presentation to give an overview of Jump's
work and our philosophy. I spent most of the time talking about
how companies needed to improve the intuition of their decision makers and how the easiest way to do that was to have
firsthand experiences with the real world. I couldn't help but
remark on how the Mercedes team had traveled all the way from

Germany to California, only to spend most of their time cooped up in a hotel conference room. If they really wanted to create cars for young Americans, I said, perhaps they should actually meet some.

My teammates then opened the conference room doors to introduce ten men and women from the Bay Area, all of whom were in their twenties. I explained that these folks had volunteered to spend time talking to Mercedes about who they were and what their lives were like. The Mercedes group would divide into teams of two. Each pair would spend time talking with a participant. I asked each team to interview their participant and find out a little bit more about them. The goal was to get to know them as people. For their part, each young person had been asked to bring along photos of things that were important to them: their home, their friends, maybe their pets. The teams had half an hour to find out more about the people they interviewed and hear some of their stories.

After a half-hour, I asked the execs to talk about how well the interview had gone. Some felt that they had gotten to know their interviewee pretty well. Others remarked that they would have liked more time to get to know their participant better. A few of their comments reflected the shock of meeting someone who didn't view the world the same way they did. Especially surprising was the fact that many of the participants didn't actually care about their cars. One or two of the participants even wished they didn't have to own a car, even though they were well-off enough to afford luxury vehicles. Up until then, nearly everyone these auto executives had ever met loved cars. As we finished capturing the initial gut reactions of our guests, we announced that it was time to begin the second part of their workshop.

Each team of executives was given two hours, fifty dollars in cash, and a map of downtown San Francisco. Their assignment was simple: Purchase a gift for the person they just met. The activity would show the executives how much they had learned about the people they had interviewed. After all, when you give a gift, it's both a reflection of who you are and who you understand the recipient to be. As such, team success would be evaluated on one criterion: how much the recipient liked the gift.

Two hours later, the teams returned with admittedly mixed results. Some teams came back with rather generic tourist knick-knacks. When I asked them why they chose to buy mementos of San Francisco for people who live in San Francisco, they admitted that this hadn't occurred to them as a problem. One team came back with a bright red fanny pack, which failed to thrill their 25-year-old participant. Other teams fared much better. One group had met with a guy named Cam who, after years working for a big Silicon Valley technology firm, was gearing up to start his own business. Our execs bought him a book on entrepreneurship. They had a little money left over, which they tucked inside the front cover as a bit of seed money for the new venture. As they described why they thought Cam would like it, it was clear that they had come to know him surprisingly well. They described in detail what it felt like for Cam to struggle with the uncertainty in his life. A few of the other execs snickered at the extra twenty bucks inside the book, but the team insisted that, when you're starting out on your own, every little bit helps. Many of the other gifts turned out to be nice, little encapsulations of the empathy that the teams had developed in a short period of time.

The point of the workshop was fairly straightforward. First, we wanted the Mercedes executives to meet some real-life Americans. Second, we wanted to get them out on the streets of a major American city, absorbing information through all of their senses. But most importantly, we wanted them to start to think differently about the cars they made. You see, on some level, a great product has to function like a great gift. It's a physical manifestation of a relationship. It's both an embodiment of who the giver is and what they think of the receiver. When you get a great gift, you can't help but feel like the other person knows you. When you get a lousy gift, you wonder if they even thought about you. The same is true for products. A great one makes you feel like someone out there gets who you are. A lousy one makes you wonder what the company was thinking—or whether it even thought at all. Maybe the company was just re-gifting something that was originally intended for someone else. Our auto executives needed to make their cars into thoughtful gifts if they wanted customers to care about them in return.

The Mercedes leaders had all walked in the door assuming that what they needed to succeed was a new set of innovation techniques. They soon concluded that what they actually needed was a new set of connections to the people they wanted to sell to. Without the memories of these relationships to guide them, any of their efforts to create new vehicles could easily go awry. They needed those memories to create gifts for their customers. The team had walked into the conference room thinking about young Americans as a customer segment to be analyzed and dissected. As they walked out, they realized that the ten people they had met were actually the most important stakeholders of their work. If Cam wasn't interested in what they came up with, their efforts would be for naught. Unless they had the courage to fight for his best interests, the resulting vehicles wouldn't connect with young Americans.

THE COURAGE OF YOUR CONVICTIONS

The trip to San Francisco gave the Mercedes team a short glimpse into the lives of the people they wanted to sell to. But the team also walked away with personal memories of why it was important to pursue this business opportunity in the first place. They had met the young people they had previously only read about in research reports, and they had genuinely started to care about them as people. In many ways, the executives' memories of their conversations would be far more resonant than any secondhand descriptions that they would read later.

Such memories can act as a guidepost throughout the course of a long project. Many promising initiatives result in mediocre products or failed businesses because the final output doesn't resemble the original spark of inspiration. This is especially true when making automobiles. Creating a new car can take an incredibly long time—five to seven years, if you want to do something really different. And the further that you get from the excitement of the original idea, the harder it is to remain true to its vision. People begin to ask for compromises. Trade-offs need to be made. Without an anchor to hold on to, it can be difficult to know which features to fight for. Memories of their young friends in San Francisco gave the Mercedes executives a reason to preserve the essence of their ideas through many subsequent trade-offs and compromises. Those memories gave them the ability to say, "It needs to be that way because that's what is right for Cam." The results of their decisions now took on a human face, and they started to develop the courage to champion their vision over the long term. They couldn't turn their backs on the folks they had met.

Throughout this book, you've seen examples of how empathy can help to uncover new opportunities when people step outside of their preconceptions and walk in someone else's shoes. But seeing an opportunity isn't the same as acting on it. To do that, you have to care. When you have a real sense of caring for someone, you become compelled to act in their best interests. More than that, you can develop a sustaining source of courage to stick with an idea over the long term. Any new initiative in a company begins with energy and passion. But after months and years of work, that energy can wane. An emotionally resonant experience fades more slowly in our memories than a well-reasoned argument. When we act according to our human impulse to care for other people, we develop the courage to stay the course.

PIXAR GOES TO THE KITCHEN

At first blush, the animated film *Ratatouille* seems like a movie for kids. After all, it's the story of an adorable rat named Remy who becomes a top-tier chef in France. Goofy as that premise might be, however, the film is grounded in the real emotions of the world's finest chefs. Not surprisingly, *Ratatouille* received both critical acclaim and commercial success. Everything about the movie feels just right, from the look of the food to the interplay between members of the temperamental and talented kitchen staff. *Ratatouille* feels real and true in a way that few other films do, let alone other animated movies.

There's a good reason for this: All those details are authentic. Brad Lewis, the producer of *Ratatouille*, apprenticed under Chef Thomas Keller in his kitchen at the French Laundry. Located in California's lush Napa Valley, the French Laundry is widely considered to be the best restaurant in America. Lewis went there so that he could learn about the chefs and cooks he wanted the film to honor. Lewis became the lowest of the low in the kitchen; he chopped vegetables, fetched ingredients, and stepped in when his more senior cooks needed his assistance. He messed some stuff up. He got yelled at. He was praised. By the time he left the restaurant, Lewis knew all the highs, low, joys, and sorrows of working as a team in the kitchen. He understood what had made him happy, and he had emotional memories of all the people around him. The resulting film is a testament to the bonds he formed with everyone else in that kitchen. Though the movie is quite funny, it also takes food very seriously because that's how the people Lewis had worked with felt about their work. In an industry that uses focus groups to try to artificially engineer emotional connections, Pixar relied on emotional experiences to craft a movie that feels true to the average viewer and feels like a caring gift to any chef.

Brad Lewis helped make *Ratatouille* a great movie by bringing his memories from the French Laundry back to Pixar's studios. Any time the film reached an ambiguous point in how it portrayed the life of a chef, Lewis knew exactly how his teammates back in Napa would respond. At any number of points, the movie could have included an additional moment of humor or sentiment that strayed from the authentic experience of being a chef. But it never did. Lewis's time at the French Laundry helped guide the film to greatness. The process behind *Ratatouille* exemplifies an important tendency of memory: Events with a strong emotional component make a bigger impression on the human brain. When a memory has an emotional charge to it, it's far more difficult to forget or ignore it. Some dismiss the human instinct to place primacy on emotional information as irrationality. Others, like Brad Lewis, know that emotional grounding based on empathy can give them a guiding beacon to stay true to their ideas despite the obstacles and challenges that arise in the course of any extended process. Moreover, empathy provides the courage to keep going forward in the face of criticism. People who are driven by empathy don't want to let down the folks they serve. There's a good reason for this: The human brain is structured to put emotion ahead of intellect. When it comes down to it, our so-called sensitive side is what gives us our strength.

As we've already seen, a significant portion of the human brain is designed to help us understand one another. Mirror neurons help us interpret the intents of those around us and understand what they're feeling. But mirror neurons don't always create a lasting and resonant impression. That requires another part of our brain, the part that connects memory and emotion. The part that's wired to care.

THE LIMBIC SYSTEM

The human brain is the result of millions of years of evolution, and its physical structure is a reflection of that development process. Think of your brain as if it were an apple. In the center is a hard core—the part with the seeds. That part of your brain was the first to develop, evolving gradually out of what was essentially just the end of the spinal cord. That small core is all the brain that modern reptiles possess, be they snakes, iguanas, or crocodiles. All higher-order creatures, including birds and mammals, also share this same core reptilian brain. It gathers information from the most basic senses: sight, touch, pain, balance, and temperature. It also makes sure that your lungs keep breathing and that your heart keeps beating. The reptilian brain helps us know when we're hungry, produces the sex drive, and even contains the most primitive of all emotions: fear. It turns out that fear is the basis for all animals' fight-or-flight response, the essential instinct that keeps them alive and out of trouble. Thankfully for us, human brains are much more than an apple core.

The outer peel of the apple is what we call the neocortex. The neocortex was the most recent part of the brain to develop. It's responsible for all manner of higher-level thinking. In lower-order mammals, such as mice, the neocortex is rather thin, not unlike an apple peel. In humans, it's a whole lot thicker. The neocortex accounts for 80 percent of the human brain. Its intricate folds of gray matter hold systems for language, symbolism, abstraction, analysis, and deduction. Among other things, our neocortex allows us to make plans, have arguments, and hold down a job. The neocortex is what makes humans so darned clever.

These two brains represent two extremes. The reptilian brain is dedicated solely to survival, whereas the outer neocortex hosts reason and higher intelligence. In between these two, however, lies the sweetest part of the apple: the limbic system. It's a collection of processors and hormone controllers that governs things like memory and emotions. It also enables us to interpret the emotions of others. The limbic system is the part of our brain that allows us to care. All mammals have limbic systems, including humans, horses, and hamsters. The limbic system allows us to travel in herds, bond with our mates, and nurture our young. Paul McCartney's neocortex is what allowed him to pen the words to "Yesterday." Our limbic system is what allows us to be moved every time we hear that classic Beatles tune.

By comparison, reptiles are literally unable to care, because they lack a limbic system. Iguanas crawl on top of each other as if they were climbing on furniture. That's because the reptilian brain of an iguana has no more attachment to its Aunt Lois than it does to a rock. Baby crocodiles have to start running the minute they hatch from their eggs, because they're in danger of being immediately eaten by their mothers. Consequences, feelings, and morality don't exist for reptiles. They're selfish and disconnected. They're too unfeeling to be great pets.

Dogs, by comparison, are called Man's Best Friend for a reason. Their limbic systems enable them to care about each other and care about us, too. Your dog can tell when you've had a bad day at work. His primitive neocortex might not understand what work is or comprehend what went wrong, but his limbic system is nearly as sophisticated as your own. And when you're unhappy, he wants you to feel better. He's also able to tell you how he's feeling. His limbic system enables him to wag his tail when he's happy or sulk when he's sad. When he's ashamed, he might tuck his tail between his legs and drag his belly on the ground to ask for forgiveness. If only people were so easy to read!

The limbic system draws together many different elements of the brain to form an overall structure for handling emotional information. Among these are two regions that have particular implications for understanding how we learn to care about other people: the amygdala and the hippocampus. The amygdala is devoted to processing our emotions and those of other people. The hippocampus is essential in the formation of long-term memories. Together, the two regions serve to help us form long-term emotional connections with other people. As it turns out, the more emotionally charged an event is, the more vivid it feels to our amygdala, which then helps our hippocampus to hold on to the event for the long term. That's why our most emotional memories are also our most vivid ones. Our brains literally encode them more forcefully than they do other data.

This is the biological root of loyalty and deeply held values and beliefs. Our minds constantly form emotional associations like this, and they're incredibly strongly held. Indeed, we're wired to connect with and care for others. The limbic system enables us to form tight bonds with friends and family members. We share emotionally charged memories with them, and they become deeply embedded into our responses over time. These associations also help us evaluate new situations. They provide us with context for what appropriate behavior looks like, how we prefer to be treated, and how to form close relationships. They help us learn to do more than understand other people. They help us learn to care.

"IT'S NOT PERSONAL…IT'S JUST BUSINESS"

Humans are a social, caring species. Our limbic brains are designed to make us curious about the feelings of other people and animals. That ability to empathize is what separates us from lower-order creatures. It allows us to communicate and collaborate with others. And it allows us to read between the lines to glean information that may not be explicitly stated.

By this standard, most companies are corporate iguanas. It's as if they've skipped right over the limbic system to grow a neocortex. Corporations are ethically neutral beasts, focused on self-preservation. They're not immoral—they're amoral. They lack any sense for the impact that their actions have on others. And that goes back to how they're structured. They have a reptilian brain to act. They have a neocortex to think. They just don't have any way to feel. Without a limbic system, companies lack any sense of empathy or courage. They're either all neocortex, analyzing thoughtfully without the motivation to act, or reptilian, caught in a cycle of fight-or-flight responses. That's deeply unfortunate, because companies are made up of people, not iguanas. And people, not iguanas, buy products and services.

Unfortunately, modern capitalism has systematically sought to suppress our need to connect with other people. Managers and economists alike encourage businesspeople to look at the data, not the people. When we show up for work, they ask us to check our humanity at the door. Get the numbers and act to maximize shareholder value, regardless of other variables. Remember, "It's not personal…It's just business."

That's a strange way to describe an activity that takes up so much of our lives. It's also not true. All business is personal. People, not machines, have their hands on the wheels of the engine of capitalism. And people, not machines, actually buy and use products and services. Anyone who's ever been a salesperson, whether in a retail store or corporate front-line sales, will tell you that commercial transactions are incredibly irrational. It doesn't matter whether you're selling teddy bears or aircraft engines. Any decision-making process that involves human beings has a personal component that often outweighs the rational. We would be wise to leverage it. And we ignore it at our peril.

BUYING STEELCASE FURNITURE

Back in the nineties, Steelcase Corporation had an interesting problem. It didn't know why people were buying its products. Steelcase is the world's largest manufacturer of office furniture. At some point in our lives, most of us have sat in a Steelcase chair or worked at a Steelcase desk, whether we knew it or not. Most office furniture is purchased by facility managers, the people whose job it is to build out and maintain an office space. Facility managers handle everything in an office, from the air conditioning to the carpet to the desks. And a lot of them buy from Steelcase.

Steelcase's marketing team tried a variety of methods to identify why the company was so successful. The company conducted a survey of thousands of facility managers to ask them, on a scale of 1 to 5, whether they purchased Steelcase furniture based on price, or quality, or service, or whatever. Despite a blizzard of information, nothing really stood out as a defining reason for why facility managers purchased from Steelcase. Finally, they asked Jump to see if we had some thoughts.

Instead of running more surveys, our team decided to hang out with the people who were involved in a furniture buying decision. We spent time hanging out with facility managers. We talked to Steelcase salespeople. We followed a few of them as they went on sales calls. We didn't ask a whole lot of specific questions. We simply tried to get people to tell us stories about what their jobs were like. We observed what was going on and tried to see if we could identify any patterns. As we listened to the stories that facility managers and salespeople told us, an interesting picture emerged.

As it happens, one of the biggest reasons why people buy Steelcase furniture has little to do with Steelcase products or prices and everything to do with how facility managers see themselves. You see, many facility managers started out in architecture school. The problem is, if you go to architecture school, you quickly realize that there are far more architecture graduates than there are architecture jobs. Unless you're extraordinarily talented, you end up going back home after graduation where you sit on your parents' couch all day and feel depressed.

This goes on for far too long. Meanwhile, your parents get more and more eager to get you off of their couch. They start looking in the classified ads to find a job for you. Eventually, they hand you an ad circled in red ink. The ad says that the local insurance company has an opening for a facility manager. After all, your parents tell you, that's kind of like architecture, right? Although you might not be totally thrilled with that job, you're more than ready to leave home, so you explore facilities management. The salary is okay, the company has a good reputation, and they have a health plan, so you give it a shot.

And you wake up thirty years later, and you're still a facility manager. Maybe you like your job. Maybe you don't. Your mandate is to pack as many people into as little space as possible. People in your company are constantly calling you to complain about their furniture or to tell you that they don't like their view. The CEO even calls to say that his wife has found an interesting pattern of carpet, and why can't we use that pattern instead of what we use now? In the midst of all these issues, you think to yourself, *But I'm an architect!* So you subscribe to *Progressive*

Architecture magazine. And you hang Frank Lloyd Wright posters on the wall. And you join Internet communities about architecture. You reinforce that you are, indeed, an architect.

Successful salespeople from Steelcase understand who you
are. They walk into your office and say, "The other people out
there are hacks. But you and me, we're architects. We get it."
The two of you talk about design for thirty minutes before even
mentioning furniture, at which point the deal is basically guaranteed. You see, to really reach facility managers, you need to
speak to how they see themselves. It doesn't matter what the
sign says on the door. In their hearts, they're architects. Steelcase excels because its products and sales techniques connect to
facility managers' aspirations. The company was winning deals
by leveraging the implicit insights of its frontline sales force. It
just didn't know it. That's wonderful for Steelcase, but it's also
the point at which traditional market research fails. How on
earth do you ask in a survey, "On a scale of 1 to 5, how much does
the fact that you're a frustrated architect affect your furniture
purchasing decisions?" You can't.

Companies presume that space efficiency and sale prices
will make facility managers sit up and take notice, but such factors miss the point. Steelcase is successful because it cares for
its customers. Its salespeople don't just sell furniture—they try
to make facility managers feel like heroes: champions of design
who also understand the strategic demands of the businesses
they support. And Steelcase prospers as a result. Facility managers aren't an unusually frustrated bunch of people; we all have
frustrations in our lives at home and at work. The companies
that can speak to our frustrations in an empathic, intuitive way
end up getting our business.

When you think about it, it seems natural that a supposedly
rational business-to-business sales process might have a human

component. After all, humans are doing the buying and selling. Yet many companies fail to take that idea into account. As a result, they leave behind valuable information that might tip the scales in their favor.

LOSING 65,000 JOBS

The key to developing real empathy, then, is to trigger an emotional response by engaging in firsthand human contact, like the Mercedes team did. Without that firsthand experience, it's often difficult for people to appreciate the importance of potentially critical information. In the United States, one of our most-watched measures of overall economic health is the jobs growth number, reported each month by the Bureau of Labor Statistics. A great month might add more than a million jobs to the economy, and a poor month might see an equal number of jobs eliminated. But as useful as this measure is for overall trend analysis, it paints an inaccurate picture of the real state of the nation. That's because it doesn't measure the number of jobs actually created or the number of jobs actually lost. For example, a month in which the U.S. economy added 50,000 jobs could actually be a month in which 100,000 people had their jobs eliminated while 150,000 other people gained new employment. While that's a net gain for the U.S. as a whole, it's impossible to tell whether it's a positive development for the nation. Were the jobs that were eliminated high paying or low paying? Were the regions that added jobs different from the ones that lost them? What happened to those 100,000 people who just lost their livelihoods?

The economy of the United States is not an academic exercise. It's a complex organism made up of real people. If I lose my job, I don't take comfort in the fact that someone somewhere else gained a job, to make the net change zero. I'm still out of a job. By focusing on net gains or losses, media reports based on labor statistics can paint a falsely optimistic vision of the economy. When they look beyond the numbers to study the people whose fortunes are actually changing, they sometimes find that the story told by the statistics is different from what's actually happening. For their part, there's little impetus for lawmakers to act without that human experience. As the old joke goes, there's only one real difference between a recession and a depression. A recession is when the guy next door loses his job. A depression is when you lose yours.

OPERATION BEAR HUG

The impetus for change often starts with a personal experience that makes us care about someone else. Unfortunately, most large organizations can't depend on a single person's experience. And creating an empathic organization can't depend on the wisdom of a single visionary leader. It needs to be widespread. That's not as hard to do as it seems. After all, every one of us is wired to care. We just need to create the kind of experiences that will trigger a caring response. Lou Gerstner's turnaround plan at IBM grew out of his experiences as an IBM customer. But that alone wouldn't have transformed the company. He needed his team to have an empathic connection as well. He also realized that his own experiences couldn't accurately reflect the sheer diversity of IBM customers. Gerstner needed a broader swath of the company to have empathy for a broader swath of its customers. That, in turn, would help everyone to make better decisions about how to create new value for IBM's customers.

In 1993, Gerstner launched Operation Bear Hug. The program required each of his fifty top managers to meet with at least five of IBM's biggest customers in the span of three months.

Managers weren't supposed to sell product in those meetings. Instead, they were to listen to customer concerns and think about how IBM might help. All of those executives' 200 direct reports then had to do the same thing. Gerstner demanded short written reports on the outcomes of each Bear Hug meeting, and he personally read every single one.

"It created quite a stir," Gerstner later recalled. "When people realized that I really did read every one of the reports, there was quick improvement in action and responsiveness."

Bear Hug immediately led to quicker actions to resolve customer problems, as well as greater attention to new market challenges. To make sure Bear Hug had a lasting effect, Gerstner started asking about it in every meeting he attended. No matter whether he was in a meeting to discuss marketing, R&D, or supply chain, he'd ask the same question: "What are customers telling us?" At first, more than a few managers were surprised by the question. They had a hard time seeing why customers might be relevant to every topic. Over time, though, Gerstner's dogged attention to the outside world started to shift the company, making it less insular, less arrogant, and more outward-looking. That empathic connection to real-world customers helped managers to see whether a particular decision added value for customers or destroyed it. It also revealed some major opportunities. Managers discovered that large corporate clients were fascinated by the Internet but unclear about what to do about it. More than just selling product, IBM realized that it could make a major impact by providing the infrastructure needed to help large enterprises leverage the power of the web. The resulting e-business initiative was wildly successful and helped put IBM on the path to long-term growth.

Gerstner credits Bear Hug with jump-starting a cultural change at IBM. He didn't turn the company around by pitching

customers on IBM products or launching a massive research initiative. Instead, the firm's leaders spent time with people and listened to their concerns. They heard stories from their lives. They
figured out how they could help. Gerstner restored an organi-
zation-wide connection to the outside world and generated
widespread empathy in the process. Initially, that connection
wasn't terribly sophisticated; it was just an overt effort to show
IBM's customers that the company cared about their needs and
wanted to work together for years to come. Over time, the entire
organization developed a deeper level of understanding for the
people that it served.

TRIGGERING THE CARE RESPONSE

The response of our limbic system is stronger when it's triggered
by face-to-face interactions. Pixar, Steelcase, and IBM wouldn't
be the successful companies they are today if they hadn't made
a sincere commitment to learn about people firsthand. That
firsthand contact provides the human context that allows the
limbic system to carefully weigh the impacts of a decision the
neocortex wants to make. In order to have the courage of their
convictions to stick with something over the long term, decision
makers need to see, hear, feel, and care about the people that
they affect. The biological mechanisms that determine long-
term memory and personal associations simply can't get too
fired up about numbers without the context needed to interpret
them. Few of us get inspired just by reading data on a page. We
need to create a fuller picture of the people involved for the benefits of emotional memory to make a difference.

Yet, as sophisticated as our neurological systems for detect-
ing the feelings of others might be, we've created a corporate
world that strives to eliminate the most human elements of

business. Companies systematically dull the natural power that each of us has to care about other people. And by dulling our impulse to care, corporations make decisions that look good on paper but do real harm when put into practice in the real world. They behave like incredibly bright but unfeeling iguanas. They make clever but selfish decisions that ignore possible impacts on other people. Fortunately, the people inside companies are not iguanas. They have feelings, and they're wired to care for one another. They just need to have that response triggered by human contact.

When we have face-to-face contact with the people we serve, our limbic systems give us the emotional context needed to help companies prosper. The challenge for companies that seek to tap this human power, however, is that one person's empathy does not automatically scale to the level of an organization. Realizing the business benefits of empathy requires companies to do more than just allow people to act human at the office. Organizations need to turn each individual's capacity to care into a shared operational resource that helps everyone to do better work. To make empathy truly widespread, we have to systematically open up an organization to the world around it.

SEVEN

Open All the Windows

While having empathy for other people is a good thing for us to do as individuals, it's far more powerful when you can create widespread empathy throughout a large organization.

EMPATHY CAN HELP make good leaders into great ones. Empathic leaders see new opportunities faster than their competitors, have the courage to take a risk on something new, and have the gut-level intuition that they need to make the right decisions when the path ahead is unclear. Any individual can do the same—the human brain is filled with structures that help us to understand and relate to other people. Fostering empathy in an entire organization, however, is much harder. The thousands of people who make up a large company inevitably accumulate implicit experiences, feelings, and insights that affect the way each of them makes decisions. But that alone doesn't scale to make an organization that has a collective, widespread sense of empathy.

Consider a company that makes accounting software. If the CEO is a former accountant, he might know intuitively how to create, market, and support products that really connect with other accountants. That doesn't mean, however, that the programmers who actually create the software have any actual understanding of accountants. When the CEO walks out of the room, the programmers still need to be able to make good decisions that serve the best interests of their customers. And that won't happen if they don't have a clear, personal sense of the people they serve. Empathy can start at the top, as it did when Lou Gerstner joined IBM, but it needs to reach everyone to have an enduring impact. How do you make the leap from personal intuition to better judgment across the board?

JACK STACK OPENS THE BOOKS

From the first day it opened, the ReNew Center in Springfield, Missouri, seemed doomed to fail. International Harvester, a leading maker of agricultural machinery, construction equipment, and commercial trucks, had established the plant in 1974 as an all-inclusive repair division. Unfortunately, International Harvester's own business began to decline soon after opening the Springfield facility. Worse, remanufacturing diesel engines, transmissions, and torque converters for construction equipment proved to be a less profitable venture than anticipated. After five years of scaling up the ReNew business, the center was still unprofitable. The operation was generating $26 million in revenue but losing $2 million each year.

Into this environment stepped Jack Stack, an 11-year International Harvester veteran who had most recently served as a manager of more than 2,000 machinists at a factory near Chicago. Stack was well known as a great motivator, and in 1979 the company's leaders had brought him in to reverse the fortunes of the renamed Springfield ReManufacturing Center, or SRC. As soon as he arrived, his approach to management made an impact. Within two years, he had made the operation marginally profitable. Stack turned a facility that was losing $2 million a year into one that made $1 million in 1981. Things were looking up.

But then the bottom fell out. International Harvester ordered SRC to cut its production by two-thirds. The parent company was struggling to make ends meet amid a wider recession for heavy equipment, and it also had a serious cash-flow problem. The larger organization could save a lot of money by idling SRC, but it would mean laying off most of the plant's employees. This was unacceptable to Stack and his team. Asking for more time and the opportunity to prove the organization's long-term potential, Stack and a group of a dozen other plant managers kept SRC working and profitable during the economic downturn. In 1982, Stack and his partners scraped together $9 million to stage a management buyout. Stack and his team were confident that they could revive the moribund unit, but they also knew that a lot needed to change at SRC to make that happen. The organization still wasn't as efficient as it needed to be.

Stack and his colleagues realized that the only way to successfully make a multitude of changes quickly was to enlist the help of every person in the company. Though the managers had a pretty clear idea of how to make things better, they couldn't implement those changes on their own. Employees needed to think and act like they owned the company. They needed to understand the business consequences of their actions and learn how to make better decisions. To achieve this, every SRC employee was taught how to read the company's financial statements, including all the numbers that were most critical to tracking business performance. Then Stack opened the books. The management team posted the company's financials on the break room walls, in employee handouts, and in other public areas of the facility. The company launched training courses and regular meetings to teach everyone how to interpret the numbers. SRC employees now had clear indicators of whether the company was making any money. They also had a better sense for how their actions as individuals affected SRC's overall performance. In the process, they helped spawn the revolution that we now call open-book management.

The effects of opening the books at SRC were immediate. Suddenly, a machinist on the shop floor could see the bottom-line impact of finishing a part faster, reducing raw material use, or shaving some time off a job. The results were astounding. SRC's sales grew 40 percent annually in the first three years following the buy-back. In the same period, net operating income rose to 11 percent. The appraised value of a share of SRC rose from 10¢ to $8.45. The owners of SRC had purchased the company for just $100,000 of their own money and $8.9 million in loans. The company was now worth several times that. Today, SRC commands more than $300 million in annual revenue and employs more than 1,000 people, up from a low of 120 in the early 1980s.

At the same time, the impact of open-book management has extended far beyond the walls of SRC. Other manufacturers heard of the company's turnaround, and they, too, overhauled their decision structures to arm their employees with the financial knowledge and power to promote productivity and cut costs. By 1995, *Inc.* magazine had devoted an entire issue to the open-book management phenomenon.

THE SUM OF A THOUSAND DECISIONS

Open-book management works because it acknowledges the power that individuals can have in the aggregate. It's precisely that insight that companies need to embrace if they want to create widespread empathy. Despite what conventional wisdom might suggest, effective corporate action is rarely the result of a single individual or a brilliant plan. In reality, it's the sum of ten thousand decisions that individuals make on a daily basis. If those decisions add up to a positive effect, the company does well. If those decisions add up to a negative effect, the company suffers. If those decisions ultimately counteract each other or try to pull the organization in opposing directions, the result is collective inaction. It's a little like a rowboat with thousands of oars in the water. To move ahead, you have to get everyone paddling in the same direction.

The emergent nature of corporate strategy was first articulated by Henry Mintzberg, one of the fathers of modern strategic planning. In his classic book, *The Rise and Fall of Strategic Planning,* Mintzberg declared that "Analysis is not synthesis, and strategic planning is not strategy formation. ...Ultimately, the term 'strategic planning' has proved to be an oxymoron." He advises us to take those plans that we spent months crafting and throw them out. Having one of the leading lights of strategic planning question its fundamental premise is a little like Mickey Mouse telling you that the rides at Disneyland are no fun. What Mintzberg really meant was that real strategy isn't some plan that gets crafted on the top floor of headquarters by a small team of high-level executives and planners. It isn't a report that a consultant delivers. Real strategy is the aggregate of thousands of decisions that employees make over time. When you improve those decisions, you improve your strategy.

Both Jack Stack and Henry Mintzberg recognize that a companywide initiative works only if you can make it meaningful to every individual within an organization. SRC was able to grow its business because it got everyone in the company to understand the financial impact of their decisions. By exposing people to better information and providing quick feedback loops, SRC made a connection between individual actions and collective outcome.

Open-book management is an effective way to help companies rapidly improve their profitability and drive revenues in an existing core business. That said, it doesn't necessarily ensure growth. Short-term financial success can't protect a company from being blindsided by new threats. Operational efficiency doesn't guarantee a firm's ability to discover and leverage new opportunities for growth. For most companies, that kind of growth depends on knowing what customers actually value. More sublime than having an open book, companies need an open channel of empathy between company and customer.

OPEN EMPATHY ORGANIZATIONS

The idea of creating an Open Empathy Organization is to build and propagate a system of human information. It's about every member of an organization having a firsthand sense of what people need, how their company solves those needs, and how what they do as individuals can add or subtract value. Open Empathy Organizations show employees the link between the products and services that they create and the people who use them.

Nike is a great example of an Open Empathy Organization. At Nike, the people who develop running shoes are usually runners themselves. They possess a basic intuition for running that can't be captured in any report. As a result, the shoes they make end up being quite good, independent of any market research. Not surprisingly, the company seeks to support this. Nike's corporate campus in Beaverton, Oregon, looks a lot like a wealthy university that decided to get rid of the classrooms and add a few more athletic centers. Cafeterias sport flat-panel televisions that broadcast athletic events from around the world. Display cases around the campus proudly feature the uniforms, equipment, and photos of famous athletes and ordinary fans. On a given afternoon, a visitor to Nike is likely to find a few employees caught up in a pickup game of soccer on one of the many fields. Employees routinely schedule in time in the middle of the day to go for a run or a swim. More than a few of the people I've met there are bright, athletic folks who found a way to channel their passion for sports into a career in business.

When employees can see that their daily activities have an impact on people outside their company, they often become inspired to create more positive impacts. Most of us are reasonably good at figuring out how to make each other happier, but those instincts can't kick in if we can't see the people we're trying to help. Widespread empathy restores that connection. That's why, just as with open-book management, people in Open Empathy Organizations make better decisions. When they can see who they're really working for, they know why their work matters and how to do it better. Instead of realizing how finishing a project faster will make the company more profitable, everyone in Open Empathy Organizations knows exactly where value resides in the world of customers and potential customers.

Creating an Open Empathy Organization isn't a market research activity. It's an issue of organizational change. Generating widespread empathy throughout a company requires the active involvement of senior leadership. It can demand changes in how employees are trained. It can call for changes in what facilities look like. It can even change how managers are incentivized. The ultimate goal is to affect the thousands of decisions that people make every day.

OPENING THE WINDOWS

A company is a lot like a building. Buildings help bring people together, protect them from the outside world, and create an environment where they can work more effectively. But the most important benefit of a building—insulation from the rest of the world—is also its greatest flaw. When you're inside a building with central heating and cooling, the temperature is perfectly tuned to be pleasant. While that makes for a nice work environment, it also cuts you off from clues about what the weather is like outside. If you have an office in the center of a building, you can't even tell whether it's day or night without checking a clock. You won't know if it's raining outside, which can lead to unpleasant surprises when it's time to head home.

Buildings can create more serious problems, as well. Many buildings constructed after the 1970s have such air-tight insulation that their occupants literally end up breathing their own fumes. These buildings simply can't pump in fresh air fast enough to get rid of the oxygen-poor air that their inhabitants exhale. It also means that when someone in an office gets sick, the people around them get sick, too. In 1984, the World Health Organization described a human epidemic created by technological advances, Sick Building Syndrome. According to the WHO, up to 30 percent of new buildings make their occupants chronically ill for reasons that can't be explained by any cause other than air-tight insulation. Quite by accident, human ingenuity has traded one kind of insecurity—vulnerability to predators, coldness and exposure to weather—for a plague of our own creation.

Before humans developed insulated forms of shelter, no one had trouble assessing the state of their environment. That's because the world inside and the world outside were basically the same place, with all the good and bad that entailed. A tiger might attack them while they slept, but no one ever got sick for lack of fresh air. The best buildings are those that protect their occupants from harm but also allow them to stay in touch with everything that lies outside their walls. They merge the best of our prehistoric existence with the best of our contemporary existence. They have lots of windows so people can see what time of day it is and what's happening with the weather. Even better, they have windows that open so anyone can get a breath of fresh air and discover how warm or cold it is outside. That same fresh air also slows the spread of illness. Any building can be made into a healthier place through constant exposure to fresh air.

Just like buildings, companies need fresh air from the outside world, too. That air comes in the form of empathic information. The Industrial Revolution exponentially increased human productivity and created a global economy. But it also severed the intuitive connection that artisans of days gone by had for their customers. This has led to a form of Sick Building Syndrome that is endemic to corporations. Most companies don't have a widespread, intuitive sense for the people they serve. Companies have created consumer research organizations to resolve this situation, but these groups can often serve to gain empathy without distributing it widely. A building is hardly flooded with fresh air if only one of its rooms has the windows open, and a company doesn't develop widespread empathy just because it has a small group devoted to studying people. Outside information has to reach every corner of the organization to make a meaningful impact on the ways people go about their work.

Throughout this book, we've had the chance to meet a few Open Empathy Organizations. Harley-Davidson fills its headquarters with tangible reminders of the shared story of motorcycle riding. Everyone who works at Harley need only look around them to understand exactly what riders genuinely value. Nike has built an entire culture to celebrate the potential for athletic greatness in each of us. IBM helps its customers to keep their information technology up and running, which is why the company stays as close as possible to its business clientele. The company uses its services division, direct sales force, and online portals to connect employees with customers on a daily basis. For these companies and firms like them, empathy is an intangible but important asset, and it's an engine for business growth.

Open Empathy Organizations outperform their competitors and consistently add value to the top line because they keep all of their windows open. More than forming consumer research groups, they create human resources systems, incentive programs, and daily work practices that translate the empathy of thousands of individuals into a widely shared, enduring source of sustainable growth. This might sound like a daunting undertaking, but any company can get started with a few small changes. Organizations that make empathy an easy, everyday, and experiential part of the way that their employees work are the ones that succeed in making empathy widespread.

MAKE IT EASY

Open Empathy Organizations depend on having employees at all levels who are genuinely interested in other people. That can be difficult, especially since no one likes to take on a bunch of extra work. Everyone has enough to do as it is—mandating ethnographic field research visits for all employees simply adds to their workload. Open Empathy Organizations don't make their employees work hard to develop empathy for their customers—they provide lots of easy ways to interact. Although every business needs to walk many miles in the shoes of their customers, few have the time or budget to travel thousands of miles to take that walk.

For this very reason, there is an actual Target store next to Target headquarters. Any Targeteer can walk downstairs, meet a few Target customers, and become a shopper himself. Many retail companies are located miles from their nearest store, which makes it hard for their employees to walk in the shoes of their customers. Target just asks you to walk downstairs.

That's not to say that Target has gotten everything right. Target shoppers tend to be middle-class folks with an appreciation for both style and low prices. When they shop at Target, they wear the casual, fashionable clothes sold at the retailer. Target corporate headquarters used to be the same way. It wasn't unusual to see executives wearing the same clothes that they helped put on the shelves. That changed in 2004 when Target created a strict dress code requiring formal business attire. Changing the dress code created two obstacles to empathy. First, Targeteers no longer looked like their customers. Second, and more important, they now had to shop at other stores to buy clothing that was more suitable for work. Local newspapers even noted a marked increase in sales for menswear stores serving Target employees in need of sharper clothes. Target later began to sell suits in its stores, but the changes had already been felt.

There are easy ways to extend an empathy program outside of the workplace, as well. Mail-order video rental service Netflix operates a simple and effective empathy program. When you start as a new coder, marketer, or even line worker at Netflix, you're given a DVD player if you don't own one. As an employee, you also get a free subscription to the company's service. As DVDs begin to arrive in your mailbox at home, you experience what all Netflix subscribers experience. You learn how to change the order of the films that you want to watch on your online queue, you anticipate the arrival of new discs, and you learn how to repackage the discs to ship them back to Netflix. People at Netflix don't have to wonder what it's like to be a Netflix customer; they've become customers, too. The Netflix service model involves many different interactions that need to work perfectly for the company to deliver value to its customers. If the wrong disc gets mailed out, the U.S. Postal Service misplaces a Netflix envelope, or if a disc isn't properly checked into the system on return, the company ends up delivering headaches, not movies, to its customers. This is why the empathy program is so important to the organization's long-term growth. When its movies take too long to ship or the wrong disc comes in the mail, employees at Netflix notice and work hard to prevent the same thing from ever happening again. Subscribing to its own service allows everyone at Netflix to see constant areas for improvement and to envision new services to add value to its existing offering.

MAKE IT EVERYDAY

At first, the novelty of empathy-building activities can make the initiative seem special, a break from the routine of work. That's a bad sign. Open Empathy Organizations avoid the kind of "big empathy-building events" that leaders love to kick off. While they can create a lot of excitement, these one-off activities rarely have lasting impact. It's far more important to insert empathic information into the workplace on a daily basis. To really stick, empathy needs to be part of the everyday routine: accessible, quick, and a constant presence.

I came across a good method for making empathy an everyday part of work several years ago while visiting Tony Salvador at Intel. Tony is a design ethnographer, which means that he spends most of his time conducting extensive interviews with ordinary people in their homes to figure out what sorts of devices Intel and its partners should create next. Empathy is incredibly easy for an ethnographer like Tony. It's literally his day job. He and the other ethnographers in his group have as strong a sense as anyone on the planet for how people are living and, especially, interacting with technology. To reach the rest of the organization, the ethnography group translates what it learns about people into end-user "personas," fictional people whose demographics, personality traits, and habits are based on those of the actual people the team met. Such personas can provide touchstones in the product development process, but they wouldn't have any impact at Intel unless people read them. That's why Intel's ethnography group has created a unique method for spreading personas throughout the organization. The team has hit upon one of the rare moments when people sit down and have some time to themselves: in the bathroom. Intel posts the personas inside restroom stalls, where they're easy to access and read. After all, people are going to spend time there anyway. Why not help them learn something in the process?

Spalding is another company that has found ways to make empathy an everyday practice for its employees. The world's leading maker of basketballs, Spalding makes a strong statement for its products at its corporate office in Springfield, Massachusetts. Right outside the building is a basketball court. Getting people onto the court is a fun, low-effort way to keep employees in touch with what it feels like to play a pick-up game of basketball. It also gives them the opportunity to experience their own products in the way they're meant to be used. Spalding is the world leader in basketballs, and anyone can dribble one to the hoop right out of headquarters. And they learn a lot when they do. For one thing, they noticed that inflating a basketball is a huge hassle, particularly because you can't just use an air pump—you need to have a needle on hand. That's why Spalding created basketballs that have tiny built-in pumps. It's the same reason the company has now created basketballs that don't need to be pumped up at all. Because they play basketball at work, people in the company are keenly aware that basketball is much more fun when you don't need to worry about a pump.

Intel and Spalding work to make empathy a set of routine and low-overhead activities that anyone in the organization can perform. Far from requiring an over-commitment of time, such practices are just part of the everyday routine of work.

MAKE IT EXPERIENTIAL

Finally, it's important to make empathic information experiential. Mirror neurons and limbic systems aren't easily triggered by PowerPoint slides and Excel spreadsheets. Open Empathy Organizations work to create ways for employees to interact with customers and environments for themselves. Sometimes that means encouraging employees to get out into the world. Other times, it means bringing the outside world into the office.

Since its founding in the 1970s, gardening tools company Smith & Hawken has consciously worked to stay close to gardeners. Part of that has meant finding ways to get outside. The company has a large garden at its headquarters in Novato, California. And it's not just for show. Everyone in the company is required to take rotations working in the garden. This is backbreaking work: hoeing, shoveling, and weeding. They get down in the dirt. Though physically grueling, this is not punishment for employees of the firm. Instead, it's the company's way of helping the entire organization to develop a better gut sense for how real gardeners view the world. Instead of spending money on focus groups, people at Smith & Hawken spend their time becoming more like the people whose business they depend on. The gardening program helped Smith & Hawken create an empathic connection that helped employees quadruple the company in size and expand from a mail-order business into one of the fastest-growing retail companies on the planet. Time and time again, Smith & Hawken employees have gone out to dig in the garden. And time and time again, the organization has grown more fruitful.

Nike is a major brand in the United States, but it's also a big name in Japan, a notoriously difficult market for American companies to crack. Experiential empathy has made this possible. At the beginning of a project for Japan, Nike designers visit the country in person to gain inspiration by hanging out with teenagers. The designers see their homes, go to school with them, and get a sense for what cool means to them. Upon returning home to Beaverton, Nike designers re-create the environments they've visited overseas. They build rooms that look like the teenagers' bedrooms they saw in Japan, right down to the posters on the walls and the color palette of the furniture. They even turn on the same Japanese TV shows that teenagers there like to watch. These rooms serve as an immersive space to help designers and marketers create offerings for Japan, whether they got to go on the trip or not. They sketch, brainstorm, and debate a product's look or positioning while immersed in the world of the people they want to connect with. Nike's designers feed their intuitions long after they've returned home to Oregon. While Smith & Hawken encourages employees to get outside, Nike works to bring the outside world in. Both companies strive to make empathic information experiential.

IT'S ABOUT GROWTH

Creating an Open Empathy Organization is a long-term process of organizational change. But the first steps toward an Open Empathy Organization are simple: Take the way that you already work today and add in easy, everyday, and experiential activities that put you in the shoes of the people you serve. This process can start with a single division of a larger organization, or even a small team, as happened when Microsoft created the Xbox. Though the benefits are remarkable when a company opens all of its windows, companies can begin to change by filling just one wing of the building with fresh air. If a single unit develops widespread empathy, that group's enthusiasm can spread to everyone else in the company. Over time, any organization can learn to hear what people outside its walls are talking about, feel what they are feeling, and see the world through their eyes. Open Empathy Organizations see the world as it really is: rich with life and overflowing with unseen opportunities to grow.

PART III

The Results of Empathy

EIGHT

Reframe How You See the World

*When you step outside of yourself, you
open up to the possibility of seeing
new opportunities for growth.*

WHEN PEOPLE in an organization have an implicit understanding of the world around them, they make a thousand better decisions every day. They're able to see new opportunities faster than companies that rely on secondhand information. And they spend less time and money arguing about things that should be intuitively obvious. Empathy drives growth because it tells an organization what's valuable to the people outside its walls. Often the benefits of an empathic organization are cumulative over time. A thousand better decisions can collectively add up to massive change. But empathy doesn't have benefits just in the aggregate. Sometimes having an empathic connection to the world around you can reveal huge opportunities that everyone else was missing. Sometimes it can reframe how you see the world.

A reframe is more than an insight or an interesting nugget of data. It's a fundamental shift in thinking about how the world works. A reframe doesn't just shed light on a situation—it invalidates previous models for how the world works. That's the reason why it can radically transform a business. Armed with the right reframe, companies can discover new value in almost any market. When you learn to see the world through a new set of eyes, nothing looks the same again.

A reframe can be a momentous, disorienting experience. That's because it's so far removed from our own expectations. It's not that a few of our assumptions are proven wrong—a reframe flips the entire world on its head. It reminds me a little of a scene from *The Matrix*. In the movie, Keanu Reeves is offered the chance to take one of two pills. The blue pill will allow him to go home and forget all that he's experienced as if it were a bad dream. The red pill will show him life as it really is. Hungry for the truth, our hero takes the red pill. Within minutes, the very nature of his world is changed forever. He awakens in a high-tech pod filled with gelatinous goo, his skin pumped full of sinister tubes. Unfathomably enormous and wicked-looking machines surround him. It turns out that the life he was living was an illusion. In reality, he and most of the human race have been attached to computers, living in a dream state while their bodies powered the machines. Everything he had known was wrong.

Keanu's shocking awakening in *The Matrix* might be an extreme case, but it illustrates what a reframe can feel like. Such an experience fundamentally alters how you view the role of your work, the people whose lives it can touch, and what really matters in the work you do. A reframe can help to uncover new ways of doing business, hidden growth opportunities, and sustainable sources of competitive advantage. But none of that is likely without empathy. The best way to discover a new way of seeing the world is to first understand how other people see the world. A reframe leads to growth, and empathy can lay the groundwork for a reframe.

THREE KINDS OF REFRAMES

A reframe has the capacity to stimulate tremendous growth and change in business, government, and education. There are essentially three kinds of ways in which you can reframe your point of view. First, you can step out of your own perspective and see the world as it sees itself. That's what happened to Pattie Moore when she experienced life as a senior citizen. Second, you can see the world in a way that's completely different from anyone else. Instead of just seeing the world the way other people do, this kind of reframe is about reading between the lines to see what's going on beneath the surface. Keanu's journey in *The Matrix* starts with this kind of reframe. Finally, it's possible to reframe the way you solve a problem. Seemingly intractable problems often become intractable because everyone approaches solving them in the same way. When Alexander the Great came to the town of Gordia, the smartest minds of his era had tried and failed to unravel the legendary Gordian Knot. Alexander took one look at the mass of string before him, pulled out his sword, and chopped the tangled mess in half. He saw a new way to solve the problem.

Understanding each kind of reframe in greater detail shows the benefits that a reframe delivers, as well as the critical role that empathy plays in its success. Any of these kinds of reframes can radically transform a business. But none of them is possible without a deep connection to people. By seeing the world through the eyes of ordinary people, companies can recognize a variety of new, interesting, and ultimately lucrative opportunities that no one has developed yet.

A reframe often happens when a company starts to see the world in the way that ordinary people do. Such a reframe can show a company how to change its business to reflect the outlook of its customers. The resulting solutions often connect in a deep and resonant way with the people whose lives inspired them. No company knows this better than Target, which has undergone just such a transformation in recent years, growing from an undifferentiated discount retailer into a leader of design for the masses.

SEEING THE WORLD AS IT SEES ITSELF

The argument starts quietly in the kitchen department of a big store outside of Detroit. Daniel is 18 years old and getting ready to go off to college in a month. Passing by a display, he reaches over and picks up an electric tea kettle. His dad is standing next to him, and he frowns. "You're not going to need that." Dad says. He looks down at the shopping list that the two made together the previous night.

"Sure I will," Daniel insists. "What if I'm studying really late at night and I need to make tea?"

"There won't be a kettle in the dorm that you can use?" his dad asks skeptically.

"There isn't any communal kettle!" Daniel says, annoyed. "Everyone needs to bring their own."

"You can buy a tea kettle any time," Dad replies impatiently.

"I can buy *any* of this any time!" Daniel fires back.

"No one will let you use a kettle to boil water in?" Dad asks.

"Look, why is this so difficult?" Daniel takes a breath and starts to speak more slowly. "If someone else brings a kettle, it's not mine to use, right?"

But Dad has already started to walk away from the display. After another five minutes of increasingly heated remarks, the father and son walk silently out of the kitchen department, leaving the tea kettle on the shelf. Daniel is frustrated, and his Dad can't seem to figure out why. Since when do teenagers care so much about tea kettles?

Back to School sales are an American retailer's best friend during the late summer months. Each year, 70 million students gear up for school. This diverse group includes both 5-year-olds starting kindergarten and 21-year-olds headed back for their senior year of college. As students prepare for a new year, retailers try to sell them billions of dollars worth of school supplies and clothing, not to mention lunchboxes, computers, and sports equipment. For retailers, Back to School is a third-quarter Christmas, driving store traffic and sales year after year.

Despite that traffic, Back to School sales remain a fairly homogenous affair. In the month of August, discount retailers in America seem to blur together into one undifferentiated mass. Whether you walk into K-Mart, Wal-Mart, or Dollar General, you'll invariably discover the same scene. The shelves are stacked high with notebooks, pencils, and backpacks. Enormous signs that look like loose leaf sheets of ruled paper hang from the ceiling with the phrase "Back to School Savings" written across them. The sheer diversity of age groups and tastes leads retailers to play it safe rather than risk excluding anyone. It's easier to just sell the same things that everyone else does.

At least, that's how it was until Target decided to change things. The second-largest retailer in the country, Target wanted to stand out from the crowd. The company had historically enjoyed better-than-average success during Back to School thanks to its focus on design, and it wanted to take things to a new level. Target wanted to do more than launch a few cool products or a fun advertising campaign. It wanted to create an entirely new approach to the season. It wanted a reframe. In search of a fresh perspective, executives contacted Jump to see if we had any ideas. And while we didn't have the answer off the top of our heads, we did have a good idea of where to start looking: at Back to School's epicenter of change.

Jump's past work had suggested that Target needed to focus on a key time of transition. Whenever our lives change dramatically, we find ourselves out of step with the world. Getting married, having a baby, moving to a new house, or even getting a dog can make our lives a little crazy. It's at those moments that we're most open to trying new things. Target needed to focus on its most interesting customers. For Back to School, that meant learning more about kids who were going off to college for the first time.

Our team spent a few weeks hanging out with families like Daniel's to understand what they were going through. We spent time in their homes, we went shopping for college with them, and we generally followed them around in the course of their daily lives. In the process, we discovered something that we didn't expect. Far from being a simple planning exercise, going off to college is an ongoing conversation. Sometimes, it's a debate. It happens between parents and students over many weeks, in short bursts, at home, with friends, and in stores. This is, after all, one of the few times in people's lives when they're buying things for a life that they haven't lived yet. Parents, for their part, haven't been to college in decades, if they went at all. To deal with the ambiguity, both students and parents make up stories about what life will be like, what the rules of the game will be, and what students will ultimately need to buy.

This is the little drama that Daniel and his dad played out in the kitchen department. As a member of our team looked on, Daniel created a story about what his life would be like that included late-night study sessions and lots of cups of tea. And it was imperative that he be prepared for that experience. After all, if he had to borrow a kettle from someone else, he might look like a loser who wasn't prepared to start college. For that matter, he might not make any friends at all. Daniel was talking about the kettle, but he was really trying to express his anxiety about a big life change. His dad had an alternate story that already imagined Daniel in a group of friends he could depend on. These two stories were in conflict. And the store was doing nothing to break the tie. It offered up a tea kettle, with no opinion whatsoever on what Daniel's life would actually be like.

We realized that Target had the opportunity to be part of the conversation—to paint a picture of college life for Daniel and other kids like him. In the process, Target could break out of the pack of undifferentiated Back to School promotions. After all, Daniel's predicament is not unique. His desire to feel ready for a new life is shared by millions of students. For Daniel, comfort came in the form of a tea kettle. For someone else, it might be a sleeping bag, a credit card, or a cell phone. What matters to any student, no matter what their age, is that they feel equipped for a big life change. And that's a very different way of thinking about Back to School. For Target, it was a reframe.

Jump worked closely with Target to help students imagine their future college life. Collaborating with designer Todd Oldham, Target offered a completely new line of products, including a lighted door sign that said either "Partying" or "Studying" depending on your mood. Besides being a fun addition to any dorm room, the sign reinforced the idea that, in college, you'd have so many friends that you might need a sign to manage your social scene.

We also tried to ease students' anxieties about striking out on their own. We created laundry bags with washing instructions printed on the inside label, so students who had never done laundry could discretely learn how without anyone else noticing their incompetence. And we even took all the kitchen tools that any student would need, from pots and pans to knives and forks, and packaged it together as a "Kitchen in a Box." Interestingly, we didn't end up including a kettle. Daniel never really needed that tea kettle—he needed the sense of readiness that it represented.

In all, hundreds of products were launched under the Todd Oldham Dorm Room brand to reflect Target's newfound understanding of the market. In the first year of the program, 2002, Target's third quarter revenue increased by 12 percent over the previous year to $8.4 billion. Wal-Mart, by comparison, remained flat, and K-Mart saw sales drop. Sales of the new products that focused most on equipping students to cope with change were up by as much as 200 percent. By really seeing the world as college freshmen did, Target realized immediate growth far beyond the incremental revenue it had hoped for. The enduring value of this reframe continued long after our initial discovery. Even five years later, in the Back to School season of 2007, Target grew by six percent while most of its competitors saw their revenues shrink. Target's reframe of Back to School from selling new stuff to delivering assurance and confidence during life changes has helped it to become the only company that consistently enjoys a merry Third-Quarter Christmas.

SEEING WHAT OTHERS CAN'T SEE

Reframing your business to reflect how ordinary people think about their lives can uncover major growth opportunities, as Target can attest. At other times, however, the greatest opportunities come from reframing the world to see what other people *can't* see about their own lives. Doing this still requires a lot of time walking in your customers' shoes and listening to the stories they tell. More than anything, though, this reframe requires the ability to read between the lines of everyday life.

It's a little bit like when you were in English class, and your professor said that Hamlet has an Oedipus Complex. Looking through Shakespeare's text, you won't find a passage that reads, "HAMLET: Gee, my mom's hot!" Hamlet's suppressed desires for his mother, the Queen, are never expressly mentioned. Still, generations of scholars have pointed to a pattern of behavior throughout the play that suggests an unspoken motivation for Hamlet's actions. Readers are left to read between the lines to understand what's really going on. Students of everyday life need to make that same leap of inference to see what others can't.

Some students take my Needfinding class because they're really interested in the subject. They're the kinds of hybrid thinkers who like to connect the needs of ordinary people with exciting new technologies and ideas for cool new products. Some students, however, take my class because it's required. As a result, I inevitably get a few students in the class who are product design majors because they care about two words: designing products. They're not very interested in caring about people, and a lot of them view product design as an opportunity to express their own creativity and aesthetics. They design for themselves.

Several years back, I had one student in particular who typified this mentality. Jeremy was an exceptionally bright guy who happened to be more interested in crafting unique forms and cool gadgets than he was in learning to care about other people. As a designer, Jeremy was great at solving problems. He wasn't as adept at discovering new problems to solve. He just seemed to be more interested in creating stuff to satisfy his own needs. That's perfectly fine—not every designer needs to be fascinated by other people. But it seemed quite clear that Needfinding wasn't going to be in a class in which he would have the opportunity to shine. After all, Jeremy and I had only ten weeks together, and that's rarely enough time for someone to fundamentally change how he approaches his work.

But Jeremy hung in there. Toward the end of the quarter, he and his classmates began to work on their final projects. Each Needfinding class has a corporate sponsor that pays for the right to have fifty of America's best and brightest try to solve one of its pressing business needs. That year, Clorox was the sponsor, which meant that all the students were studying the different ways that people think about cleaning. The students watched how senior citizens clean, how young people clean, how Latinos clean, and how suburban moms clean. We even sent students to the San Francisco Airport to watch how workers clean airplanes after a flight. The various teams started to come up with insights about how cleaning was changing in America and what that could mean for the future of Clorox's business.

Jeremy was part of a team that was studying how teenagers and college students clean. To the surprise of no one, his team saw that teenagers don't do a particularly great job of cleaning. They sweep up whenever they notice a problem, but they don't make a habit of keeping their spaces clean in the first place. Often, they push things out of sight to avoid grappling with the real messes; they wait to act until they're facing a disaster. When his team presented its findings in class, the grading panel included a vice president from Clorox. As Jeremy talked through the uninspired cleaning habits of teens, she interrupted him. "Wait a minute," she said. "It sounds like people your age don't care about cleaning nearly as much as people my age do, and Clorox should just forget about making products for you!"

Jeremy paused thoughtfully and then responded, "No, that's not what I'm saying at all. I'm saying that people tend to view the world through different frames, basic rule sets that they learn over time through their past history and experiences. And for cleaning there are two major frames at play. Some people view the world as being filled with durable goods. They presume that computers, tables, chairs—all of the stuff they buy—will be around for a long time, so they work to preserve them and keep them looking good. There's another group of people, however, who view their surroundings as inherently disposable. If they get a scratch on a table, that's no big problem to them. Why not just throw it out and get a new table?"

Jeremy continued, "Here's the problem for Clorox. Everything that you make speaks to a durable goods mentality. It says 'Keep it looking like new, return it to the way it was the day you bought it, keep it in the original condition.' That's fine for your current customers, but there is an entire generation of folks who are coming up, who think, 'Why would I keep it looking like new? Why wouldn't I throw it out and get a new one?' Your approach to cleaning works right now, but it's irrelevant to your next generation of customers."

This was a huge reframe for the Clorox vice president. She had come into the class thinking that her business was about cutting cleaning time in half, increasing antibacterial efficacy, or adding pleasant smells like lemon, lavender, and orange to her products. Jeremy helped her see the world in an entirely new way. The world was divided into Durable Goods People and Disposable Goods People. This was an idea that the folks Jeremy had interviewed could never have articulated, either. No one had said it out loud, but it was beneath the surface of every story they had told. If Clorox didn't do something for people with the disposable goods frame, its business would suffer in the long term.

Jeremy struggled with Needfinding for most of our time together, but we ended up giving him an A in the class. He earned that A in just ten minutes because he learned how to discover something that no one else could see. By uncovering the implicit frames around cleaning that different groups have, he showed the role that a different category of products could play for Clorox. For months after the presentation, I found myself walking around, classifying the people I met: *durable goods person...disposable goods people*.... Suddenly, the random behaviors of the people I knew actually made sense. There was a reason why a college buddy of mine was still holding on to his twenty-year-old VCR and why another friend bought a whole new wardrobe every year. Jeremy had helped me to see the world with new eyes.

SEE A NEW WAY TO SOLVE A PROBLEM

The first two kinds of reframing focus on empathy, understanding how other people view the world, both explicitly and implicitly. The final type of reframe, however, relies equally on creativity and empathy. Some people have a particular gift for seeing how to solve a problem differently than anyone else. Through their deep understanding of people and their own ingenuity, they're able to create new kinds of products, point to new directions for development that others can't see, and discern between ideas that are merely novel and those that are truly meaningful.

Few people have embodied the ability to reframe a solution better than the late John Rheinfrank, a design strategist whose work touched many companies throughout the 1980s and 1990s. He was also a mentor of mine. His designs were effective, clever, and deceptively simple. Rheinfrank's work often matched what people really needed so well that it was hard to believe no one had thought of it before. His ideas were so insightful that they often felt obvious.

In the mid-1980s, the Eastman Kodak Company found itself in a quandary. The photo chemicals and film manufacturer faced aggressive competition from overseas rivals that were producing new products at a pace and price that Kodak couldn't match.

Internally, Kodak engineers grew increasingly demoralized, as their annual performance was measured on the ability to shave an eighth of a cent off the cost of a roll of film. The company found itself in a game of catch-up, trying to move quickly in an industry that no longer played to its strengths. To add insult to injury, this was an industry that Kodak had invented.

Facing dim prospects, Kodak decided to change the game completely. It hired a design firm led by Rheinfrank to discover whether Kodak could differentiate itself without competing solely on price. Rheinfrank's job was to find new opportunities for Kodak to create value for its customers. The results were astounding. Most consumers believed that the company made cameras, even though Kodak hadn't made a camera in years. Many associated Kodak with photo-developing services, even though that business had been outsourced. Most important, customers associated Kodak with a whole group of activities that surrounded the use of photographic materials. Kodak thought it was in the business of making film. The average American thought Kodak was in the business of taking pictures. This opened up Kodak's prospects to ideas beyond film. It also demanded that the company start paying more attention to the role pictures played in people's lives.

To ensure its future success, it was critical for Kodak to leverage this new insight that it had gathered through empathy for ordinary people. The company needed to turn photography from an abstract process to one that was deeply embedded into the contexts where people wanted to take pictures. Taking cues from new Japanese innovations, the company introduced the Fun Saver, a disposable camera. The product was basically just a box of film with a plastic lens and an advancing mechanism. But to consumers, it was much more. It was a tool for capturing their most cherished memories. To emphasize that point and show its willingness to help people capture even better memories, Rheinfrank recommended that Kodak make a waterproof version of the Fun Saver to be sold at the beach. Kodak made a panorama version that was sold at the Grand Canyon. Kodak even made multi-packs specifically designed for weddings.

Kodak combined its newfound understanding of people with its established association with photography. This allowed them to redefine what film could be, and thereby build an entirely new category. The Fun Saver, in turn, led Kodak's transformation from being a manufacturer of film to one deeply tied into the lives of ordinary people. Kodak surpassed Fuji as the market leader for disposable film cameras.

Just a few years later, Kodak would once again face a major threat, this time in the form of digital imaging. Even though Kodak was the first company to develop a digital camera, it failed to embrace the opportunity. The company was slow to let go of its dying film business and migrate to the new technology. Ironically, Kodak might have found itself in a better position if it had held onto Rheinfrank's reframe. Kodak's business was ultimately about the pictures, not the film.

A REFRAME CAN TRANSFORM A BUSINESS

Each of the three kinds of reframes holds the potential to radically transform a business. Whether learning to see the world as it sees itself, discovering a view of the world no one else has seen, or seeing novel ways to solve existing problems, companies derive tremendous benefits from a major shift in perspective. A successful reframe demonstrates what a company knows about the world that no one else does. Though not always essential for market success, reframes are more proprietary and defensible than many other approaches to differentiation. If a company becomes successful by making cool new products, any competitor can step in and begin to knock off its design. Innovative marketing techniques are easy to duplicate. Even operational efficiencies are easily imitated. A reframe is much harder to copy, if only because it can take a while for competitors to discover what you know. They're more likely to see your actions as confusing or even misguided. They have yet to see the world like you do.

Having a unique view of the world has the potential to help any organization thrive in the long term. But as useful as any reframe can be for an organization, it can be even better to have multiple reframes at once. Having a unique view of the world can be unbeatable when you have an equally unique view of what to do about it. Dave Schenone at Nike routinely demonstrates the power of multiple reframes.

REFRAMING SPORTS CASUAL

Nike shoes make you faster. That's the value that University of Oregon track legends Phil Knight and Bill Bowerman set out to deliver when they began to sell running shoes out of the trunk of Knight's car in the 1960s. No matter where you are as an athlete, Nike would help you reach your peak performance. The look of the shoe isn't important; results are. Nike as athletic catalyst proved to be an incredibly powerful message for the fledgling company. By 1980, eight years after introducing its iconic track shoe to retail, Nike commanded a majority of the market share for athletic shoes, without making much of an advertising effort. Pushing athletic performance before all other values helped Nike to grow at an astounding rate.

But strategies can become so successful that they start to slow an organization down. Nike's dominance of the performance footwear business leaves it with less and less room to grow. When you're the number one athletic company in the world, there are only so many people left who aren't already buying your shoes. That's the challenge Dave Schenone and his team at Nike tackle every day. In search of new opportunities, he's obsessed with where the next generation of young athletes might take the Nike brand.

One day in the late 1990s, Dave was out on one of his many visits to college campuses when inspiration struck. He had come to campus to learn more about why college students weren't buying as many running shoes as they used to. Walking around, Dave noticed that almost everyone he saw was wearing baggy jeans, so big that they almost dragged along on the ground. The jeans themselves were not interesting to him; college kids always wear jeans. What caught Dave's eye was what those jeans did to shoes. They swallowed them up. Dave couldn't tell if anyone he saw was wearing Nike running shoes because the hems of the jeans were obscuring their profile.

Most college campuses are spread out enough that students need to cover great distances to get from class to class. For a long time, college students had worn jeans and tennis shoes to class in part because they were really comfortable for walking. But as Dave looked around, he saw that everyone was wearing Doc Martens boots: heavy, hot, inflexible clodhoppers that can make a mile's walk feel like two. Dave couldn't quite tell what was going on yet, but he knew that he had stumbled onto something big.

As Dave thought about what he was seeing, the reason that running shoes had fallen by the wayside on college campuses suddenly hit him. They didn't look good with baggy jeans. College students love to express their sense of identity through what they wear. The problem was, no one could see the cool shoes you were wearing under those big baggy jeans unless your shoes were just as bold and brash. Doc Martens might not be ideal for walking to class, but they were every bit as in-your-face as baggy jeans.

The inspiration came quickly to Dave: If Nike made a bold, eye-catching shoe that was designed for a variety of activities— walking to class, going for a quick run, and wearing to parties— Nike could make a new splash on campus. These wouldn't be shoes for folks who were obsessed with sports or performance; they would be for people who appreciated the look and feel of sports gear as fashion. Nike could once again rule college campuses. All it needed to do was reframe its business from making sports gear to making the gear of sports culture. That shift would open up an entirely new category for Nike. Dave had a proposition that couldn't possibly miss, except for one tiny detail: Nike didn't do casual footwear.

"If you mentioned the word 'fashion' at Nike, it was blasphemy," Dave recalls. He knew that Nike had tremendous opportunities ahead if he could help it enter the fashion business on its own terms. But the idea was an oxymoron. Nike had no terms with fashion. Nike made performance athletic gear. The opportunity Dave had seen was, on its face, a nonstarter. Nike would never go for it. Still, Dave couldn't turn his back on the opportunity. Perhaps there was a way to meet the needs of college students while making the project acceptable to Nike. After all, he just needed to come up with a shoe that met Nike's high standards for performance while also meeting college students' high standards for fashion. How hard could that be?

BLACK IS THE NEW BLACK

Looking for an answer, Dave headed to New York. Every February, New York City turns into the fashion capital of the world.

Bryant Park fills with tents where the world's leading designers, models, and paparazzi present and capture the newest looks at Fashion Week. Though held in the middle of winter, the brightly colored festival offers a reminder that spring is right around the corner. It was into this environment that Dave and his team landed. They had traveled across the country in search of a new understanding of fashion that could fit Nike's frame of performance athletics. What they found instead was a fashion world on autopilot.

"There was a phenomenon of black everywhere," Dave recalls. "Window displays were black on black. You had a black suit, a black shirt, a black tie and even a black glossy handkerchief in your pocket. On the streets, everything was black. This was weird."

Looking at New York's uniformly black fashions, Dave had a second reframe: People were going to become interested in bright colors again, soon. Done right, an eye-popping shade of orange or green could be a powerful accent to an all-black outfit. Nike could be on the leading edge with a line of shoes that came in a wide variety of colors. Unfortunately, this reframe didn't solve Dave's bigger problem: getting Nike onboard. It appeared to make things worse: Shoe stores were even more opposed to bright colors than Nike was to associating itself with fashion. Shoe stores live and die by the SKUs they carry. Short for stock-keeping units, SKUs are industry shorthand for individual variations of the products that stores put on their shelves. If one type of product comes in five sizes and two colors, stores have to stock ten separate SKUs to offer the full range of options. Stores work as hard as they can to keep SKUs to a minimum because if they carry too many, the cost of inventory goes through the roof. Worse, if stores spread their inventory too thin, they increase the chances that they will stock products no one will buy while also reducing the likelihood that they will be able to meet demand for popular products. Stores work to stock exactly enough SKUs to capture everyone's attention, and not one more.

Shoes, in particular, have a huge number of SKUs. Stocking just one color of shoe requires stores to invest in 13 separate SKUs for each of the half sizes between 7 and 13. With so many sizes, stores hate to carry more than three colors. Consumers might be interested in Dave's vision for eye-popping casual running shoes. There was even a slim possibility that he could get Nike to invest in the idea if he could show the executive team that the stylish shoes could also be performance athletic shoes. But with a myriad of colors, there was no way that retailers would ever stock the new shoes.

From the viewpoint of a shoe designer, Dave Schenone had an impossible brief. No running shoe in history could do everything that he needed this new model to do. Shoes aren't the only products that run up against stores' unwillingness to stock a large number of SKUs. So Dave looked beyond shoes. Searching for a solution, he discovered an advanced concept that Nike engineer Tobie Hatfield and designer Kevin Hoffer were experimenting with. Tobie and Kevin had found a product category in which store owners were more than happy to stock a full rainbow of colors: the T-shirt. What is it about T-shirts that makes them acceptable to retailers when brightly colored shoes are shunned? Simple sizing. While a typical running shoe needs 13 different SKUs for even one color, T-shirts get restricted to small, medium, large, and extra-large. So, while stocking three colors of running shoe in 13 sizes meant carrying 39 different SKUs for a shoe store, that same store could carry 10 different T-shirt designs in four different sizes and still end up with only 40 SKUs. The answer was to make shoes that were like T-shirts. This was a third reframe for Dave. The challenge wasn't to create a casual shoe that performed like a running shoe; it was actually to make a shoe that came in dramatically fewer sizes than the status quo. If the size could be reduced, he could get stores to carry many more colors.

Dave's explorations had revealed multiple new ways to see the world. First, while Nike thought of itself as being in the business of sports performance, there were millions of people who actually saw sports as more of a lifestyle. Second, in an age when people were only wearing black, a company that made bright colors could actually stand out. Third, the way to get more color choices into the market was to make shoes that were sized like T-shirts. He had seen the world as it saw itself. He had seen a shift that no one else could see. And he had seen a new way to solve a seemingly intractable problem. Armed with these three reframes, everything quickly fell into place.

Nike designer Bob Mervar refined the initial advanced concept to create a unique, stretchy shoe that would shrink a little to fit feet smaller than its natural size or expand to fit people whose feet were a bit too big. Using just five sizes, labeled extrasmall, small, medium, large, and extra-large, the company could fit the vast majority of people that a full range of sizes normally would. That problem solved, the design team created eight individual colors, from white and black to bright red, orange, and green. They called the concept the Nike Presto, available in a range of "magic colors."

The team still needed to prove that the Presto was a serious running shoe. So they loaned prototypes to stakeholders at Nike, including CEO Mark Parker, to show them that Presto worked as both a running shoe and a casual shoe. The executive team went running, loved the experience, and vowed to take the product to market aggressively. Parker himself declared that retailers would need to stock all eight colors of the Presto in all five sizes, or they wouldn't be allowed to sell any of the Presto line at all. Taking on the full line would require stores to order only 40 SKUs, about the same as stocking three colors of any other shoe model. As a result, every major sports running store agreed to carry the full Presto line. As soon as it launched in 2002, Presto was an overnight sensation. Runners started to wear them, proving that the shoe's performance was credible. People started buying two or three pairs at a time in multiple colors, proving its fashion appeal. And every major athletic shoe retailer bought the full line, emphasizing the success of the sizing strategy. Most important, kids on college campuses across the country began to wear the Presto to class.

Nike had created the impossible: a fashion-forward performance running shoe. The Presto also launched a new product category for the company: Sport Culture. Before Presto, Nike refused to contemplate a fashion play. After Presto, everyone at the company saw how they could make gear that was stylish *and* high performance. Following Presto's launch, the Sport Culture category grew rapidly into one of the largest business segments in the company.

None of Presto's impact would have been felt if Dave hadn't experienced his first reframe on a college campus years before the Presto took hold. By first having empathy, Dave and team were able to see a new opportunity to create a significant new category at Nike. For all the technical and business innovations he helped create with Presto, he never would have even gotten started if he hadn't been so interested to know what was going on with college students. Empathy led to reframe after reframe after reframe. Empathy also gave the team the courage to continue the project in the face of huge obstacles. Dave knew that he was on the right track because he had seen those students for himself.

Reframes are powerful vehicles for an organization's growth. They help companies rethink their value propositions, reinvent existing categories, and even redefine their business. When a company spots a reframe, it can move very quickly in a new direction. But reframes don't happen by accident. Empathy can point the way to a major reframe. If a reframe is the fundamental change that you can see, empathy is the sensor that allows you to feel that reframe before you can see it. Empathy is the necessary ingredient that precedes massive growth and change. Empathy helps make sure that you're in the right place at the right time to discover your next big growth opportunity. And the more you develop empathy for ordinary people, the easier it becomes to put yourself in their shoes. The more time you spend with the people you serve, the more the line between producer and consumer begins to blur. Eventually, you can see that your company is part of something much bigger than itself: the rest of the world.

NINE

We Are Them and They Are Us

*When companies create an empathic connection
to the rest of the world, a funny thing starts to
happen. The line between outside and in, between
producer and consumer, begins to blur.*

BETSEY FARBER loved to cook. She and her husband, Sam, would spend hours in the kitchen, transforming fresh ingredients into mouth-watering feasts. But as she grew older, cooking became harder and harder. Betsey developed a mild case of arthritis in her wrists. Though the joint pain wasn't severe, it still hurt whenever she grasped a knife or needed to hold down a cucumber for chopping. Betsey could still cook, but it wasn't as pleasant anymore.

One day in 1988, the pain became so bad that Betsey wondered if she might have to give up cooking altogether. The couple had rented a house in Provence for two months, and they planned to spend much of their time living an idyllic country life. Cooking was a big part of that life. One day, Betsey was trying to peel a potato. The peeler she held, though elegantly crafted with a sharp steel blade, wouldn't work properly. The peeler kept twisting in her hand. Moreover, it hurt to hold the potato. She wasn't getting very far, and it was clear that she wasn't going to. Seeing her distress, Sam took the potato and quickly peeled it for her.

The incident really bothered them. And the more Sam and Betsey talked about it, the angrier they became. Sure, Betsey's hands weren't as capable as they had been in her youth, but why should that mean that she couldn't cook for herself? Besides, the peeler didn't feel very comfortable in Sam's hands, either, and he didn't have arthritis. Sam and Betsey began to wonder: What if the problem wasn't them? Maybe Betsey's frustrations with the veggie peeler were less about her arthritis and more about the poor tools she was trying to use. Maybe the real problem was that the designers who made the peeler weren't designing with people like Betsey in mind.

Most people who have an experience like Sam and Betsey Farber's just end up frustrated. But the Farbers were not most people. Sam had been the founder of COPCO, a designer cookware company. His father had owned Sheffield Silver. His uncle Simon had founded Farberware back in 1900. Sam and Betsey were the heirs to a cookware dynasty. Creating products for the kitchen ran in the family. The Farbers realized that if they designed new kitchen tools that Betsey could use, a lot of other people might find them useful as well.

Sam called up his friends at Smart Design, an industrial design firm that had gained a reputation for creating products that were both aesthetically pleasing and easy to use. Sam had collaborated with Smart while still at COPCO, and he knew that they would be able to create a product line that was as elegant as it was functional. He didn't know that Smart had been sharing studio space with Pattie Moore. By then, Pattie had developed a bit of fame for her groundbreaking work walking in the shoes of elders. Pattie had continued her work as a designer, focusing her attention on opportunities to make life better for people as they age. And now Pattie worked right next to the Smart guys. Given the project, she didn't need a lot of cajoling to join the team. As

Pattie began to reflect on the Farbers' goal, she found herself transported back to a painful scene from her childhood.

Pattie had grown up in Buffalo, New York, during the booming industrial years that had followed World War II. As a child, many of her happiest days were spent in the kitchen, helping her grandmother make Sunday dinner. Because Pattie was so interested in everything, her grandma would often hand her a wax paper sack filled with M&Ms to keep her occupied. This ensured that Pattie would be too distracted to cause mischief in the kitchen. Pattie would spend hours at the kitchen table, talking with her grandmother as she arranged her M&Ms into colorful mosaics.

One particular Sunday afternoon, the duo had fallen into a familiar pattern. Grandma bustled about the kitchen stirring, baking, roasting, broiling, and simmering, while Pattie played with her candies. Remembering a forgotten ingredient, Grandma walked to the refrigerator and tugged at the handle. Though she hadn't seen what happened, Pattie froze in midsentence as her grandma let out a strange noise—a yelp, or maybe a cry. When she looked up, all that Pattie could see was her grandmother pulling her hand away from the still-sealed refrigerator and gingerly placing it underneath her other arm as she walked out of the kitchen.

"Grandma?" Pattie called softly to her grandmother. Receiving no reply, Pattie ran to her mom for help. Pattie couldn't hear what was said between Mom and Grandma as they disappeared into a bedroom, but she could just make out their muffled voices and tears. When Pattie's mom re-emerged a few minutes later, she calmly put on an apron and finished making supper. The family ate in silence and didn't talk about what had happened. In fact, they never referred to the incident again until after Grandma's death, which came less than a year later. No longer able to cook for her family, Pattie's grandmother faded quickly. "It was as though someone had pulled the plug," Pattie later recalled.

Her grandmother's awful cry stayed with Pattie as she grew older. It haunted her. Moreover, it drove her. And now, ten years since she had first made herself into an old woman, Pattie was presented with a golden opportunity to make cooking easier for elders. More than that, in collaborating with the Farbers and Smart Design, she had the opportunity to restore dignity and independence to a generation of people that had been ignored by an entire industry.

Working together with a Smart Design team led by Tucker Viemeister, Pattie and the Farbers began to explore what could be done to change the sad state of kitchen gadgetry. They performed extensive research into dexterity and its limitations. They observed people with arthritis as they struggled to use basic kitchen tools. With Pattie's help, the team conducted a Moccasins exercise to experience those challenges for themselves. They struggled to prepare dinner while wearing gloves to reduce their sensitivity, and they bound their joints so they couldn't flex as much as usual. Everyone involved in the project came to understand what life was like when your hands didn't work the way you wanted them to.

As they began to mock up possible solutions, the team zeroed in on the handles of kitchen gadgets as a significant problem that needed solving. Most existing handles were slender and tapered, to be held between the thumb and fingers instead of truly gripped. Worse, most of them became slippery when wet. In response, they created a thick rubber handle that you could grip with your whole hand. The handle had an oval shape, which made it virtually impossible to rotate by accident. Then they put that same handle onto each of fifteen different utensils, including veggie peelers, whisks, and measuring spoons. Here, at last,

were tools for Betsey to make dinner with ease. More importantly, the designers wanted to use these tools themselves.

The Farbers formed a new company to market the kitchen
tools and called it OXO, just like the little hugs-and-kisses letters that folks sometimes put on a note to a loved one. To the
Farbers' delight, the first OXO Good Grips tools were an instant
success. And the products were popular with more than arthritis sufferers. People of all ages and abilities began to buy OXO
peelers and whisks. Though the tools were designed for people
like Betsey, a lot of other people thought they were great, too.
The company grew rapidly, expanding its line to more than 500
products.

BLURRING THE LINES

The OXO team discovered one of the most fascinating effects of
widespread empathy. When people consciously reach outside of
their perspective to connect with others, something profound
starts to happen. The line between them and the outside world
gradually begins to blur. Creating Good Grips wasn't an act of
pity. In fact, it started with a fairly self-interested motive. Betsey
Farber wanted to keep cooking. Over time, though, by walking
in other people's shoes, the team realized that all of us have the
same basic needs. They could have instead designed a custom
set of tools for Betsey. Worse yet, they could have designed a
range of awful geriatric devices for the elderly. Instead, they
made something universal.

OXO succeeded because the Farbers didn't try to make
kitchen tools for old people. They made tools for *all* people. As
they developed the Good Grips products, the team spent a lot
of time talking about its approach. Pattie, the Farbers, and the
designers at Smart all realized that they couldn't design kitchen

tools just for Betsey. While she had been the inspiration for Good Grips, the idea was much bigger than her alone. They instead needed to create products that everyone could use. The team came up with the term Universal Design to describe their philosophy.

Looking back, Pattie can't help but be reminded of how other designers in Raymond Loewy's Studio had told her to forget about people like her grandmother. "Pattie," one designer had said, "we don't design for those people." OXO was proof positive that they didn't need to design for "those people." They needed to design for all people. Ironically, the Good Grips products are the sort of slick designs that the Loewy boys would have loved.

The OXO team succeeded because it exemplified something many other designers had missed: Different kinds of people aren't strange groups to be studied or categorized. They're folks like us. Today, OXO works hard to remind itself of that fact. In its New York offices is a wall covered with hundreds of lost gloves, all hanging in neat rows. The gloves range from fashionable ladies' gloves to construction workers' gloves to children's mittens. Whenever OXO employees find a lost glove on the street, they bring it into the office and hang it on the wall. It serves as a reminder of all the different kinds of people and all the different kinds of hands that OXO products need to fit.

Many companies follow this same evolution, from solving their own needs, to asking others what they want, to finally tapping into a mission with far wider relevance. Often a firm is started by an entrepreneur who creates something for herself. She caters to her own needs. If she's lucky, she soon finds that other people share those needs as well. She's able to build a company. As long as she's there, the company can enjoy a focus and clarity that other firms might lack. However, to remain successful, most companies eventually need to become less reliant on

their founder's singular vision. They discover that their charismatic founder isn't always an accurate reflection of the rest of
the world. Sometimes she's right, and sometimes she's wrong.
People worry about whether the company can outlive its founder.
Investors start clamoring for something more reliable.

At that point, companies start to establish methods for figuring out what the rest of the world wants. They gain a broader set
of opinions to help mitigate the risk of being wrong. But they
often lose their clarity and passion in the process. If they stop
there, companies can soon find that they're asking people what
they want without really knowing *why* they want it. They have
understanding without empathy. That can result in a lot of really
awful solutions. People start making geriatric kitchen devices
that they themselves would never think of buying. They shrug
and say that this is what the customer wants. They have some
understanding of the outside world, but they still view that
world as a weird place, populated by people who are not like
them. That's a dangerous situation for a company to be in. And
it's where most companies end up.

It's only when you reach outside yourself that you can see the
rest of the world as something other than a strange and confusing place. You discover that you have things in common with
other people that you didn't know. You cease to be mystified by
their purchase behavior. When you connect with other people,
a funny thing starts to happen. Over time, the line starts to
blur. Between you and them. Between producer and consumer.
Between inside and out. Suddenly, the rest of the world doesn't
look like a bunch of strangers. It looks like you. As Lara Lee at
Harley-Davidson so aptly put it, "We don't think about how we
can sell more stuff to customers. We think about how we can
better serve riders. Because at the end of the day, we are them
and they are us." When the lines between you and the rest of the

world begin to blur, the results can be profound. That usually doesn't happen overnight. But the transition can be a journey of transformation.

MIKE KEEFE LIVES IN TWO WORLDS

From the moment he finished high school until the day he received his bachelor's degree ten years later, Mike Keefe had three constants in his life: carpentry, class work, and motorcycles. During the warm months, his weekdays followed an exhausting pattern. He would wake at dawn, several hours short of a good night's sleep. He'd ride his motorcycle to whichever construction site his crew was working on, and then he'd pound nails and raise roofs from sun-up until 3:30 in the afternoon. When the whistle would blow, Mike would race home on his motorcycle, take a quick shower, put his dog into his truck, and start the 30-mile drive to night school. He'd return home hours later, bone-weary and scatter-brained. Mike would then do homework until he couldn't stay awake any longer. And each dawn, the cycle would repeat.

Mike didn't much like his life in the night school and carpentry days. But he knew that an education could open up a wealth of opportunities for him, so he pressed on. He was in night school because he wanted to make his dad proud and because he wanted to make something of himself. He was trying to live up to the values he had been raised with.

To Mike's disappointment, graduating from night school didn't actually offer a great deal of improvement. He took his first job with an ad agency in Detroit that served Dodge. In a lot of ways, this felt like going back to square one. Mike's first manager was an 18-year-old fresh out of high school. Mike had to wear a suit and tie, which made him feel like he had to put on someone else's costume just to live his own life. Still, it was a step up. At least he was working in an office with indoor bathrooms.

Though it was a jump from night school and construction, the agency job was nothing to write home about. Mike didn't drive a Dodge himself, so he didn't feel like he had a personal connection to his work. Still, he learned a lot about the demographics Dodge was trying to reach, and he did his best to tailor his work to match what he read about them. Mike did a good job of coming up with advertising messages that made Dodge's cars and trucks seem more appealing to consumers. Even so, it was hard for Mike to see any larger meaning or impact to the ads he was helping to create. It was just work. That's pretty much how Mike's life went for several years until one day in 1984, when he got a surprising phone call at his office. To his disbelief, a voice on the other end of the line asked him if he would consider interviewing to be Harley-Davidson's advertising manager. This was a dream come true. Mike's Harley had been his companion throughout his night school years. It had kept him sane through an exhausting decade of hard labor. And now Harley-Davidson wanted to meet him? It didn't seem real.

After recovering a bit from his shock, Mike answered, "Sure!" Though he had purchased his first suit and gone respectable, Mike was still a rider at heart. His continued membership in the tribe of Harley was a point of pride, so maybe it was time to join the inner circle. Still, Mike was a little skeptical. Harley-Davidson was in trouble. The company's sales had plummeted, and it was losing money at an alarming rate. Harley was headed for bankruptcy. If he were going to work there, he needed to adjust his expectations. "I basically thought, I'd like to get in 30 days and a business card that said 'Harley-Davidson' on it to prove that I'd worked there," he says looking back.

Mike drove from his home in Michigan to the company's headquarters in Milwaukee to meet with the head of marketing. He wore his "three-piece stupid suit" so he could make a good first impression, and he respectfully answered all the questions that came up in the interview. He thought he was doing well, but he also thought that he didn't have a prayer of getting the job. As his interview started to wrap up, the marketing manager looked up from her desk and asked if he had any other questions. "Yeah," he said quickly. "Could I maybe meet Willie G?"

Willie G. Davidson was a grandson of a Harley founder and a legend in the rider community. He had become a cult figure by reinventing the design of Harley's motorcycles to reflect the culture of bike customization that had developed in California during the 1950s. Willie had also watched Harley-Davidson get acquired by AMF in 1969. Soon after, Harley started to transform into a typical corporation with little connection to riders like him. Eager to get the company back to its roots, Willie G and twelve other managers bought the company back from AMF in 1982. The new owners planned to place a renewed emphasis on the company's commitment to supporting the freedom of the open road for its riders. Unfortunately, the U.S. economy was in a severe slump in the early 1980s, and those plans hadn't taken off quite yet. But Harley's leaders still had a dream and a loyal group of riders that needed them. That's why Mike was interviewing at Harley. He wanted a piece of that dream. Mike had to see Willie G while he had the chance. Mike's interviewer picked up her phone, dialed, and said, "Hello, Bill? There's someone here who would like to meet you." She hung up. "Walk right over to the other building, Mike. He'd love to see you."

Mike drew up his strength and walked across the narrow courtyard that separated the two main buildings. He started to climb the famous stairs above the "No Cages" sign when he was overwhelmed by the gravity of the situation. "I had a near-mystical experience," Mike says. "I was walking in their footsteps," following the path of the men and women who had begun Harley more than 80 years before. Passing through the lobby, Mike knocked on an office door bearing Willie G's name. The door opened, and there he was: Willie G, in the flesh. To Mike's delight, he wasn't wearing a suit. "Come on in," Willie said, as he threw an arm around Mike's shoulders and welcomed him to the inner sanctum.

Over the course of the next hour, the two men talked about everything that mattered: motorcycles and the fascinating people who ride them. Mike and Willie G had never met, but they connected deeply over their shared passion. They started swapping stories about riding motorcycles. Willie told Mike about how custom motorcycles were really a form of folk art. People didn't paint images of epic hunts on cave walls anymore, but they still painted their gas tanks and added new handlebars to their motorcycles to show who they were. Warring tribes no long captured the flags and emblems of rival clans, but groups of riders still liked to wear patches and T-shirts that showed off their affiliations. For Harley-Davidson riders, motorcycles had become a canvas for their personal identities. And the company, in turn, needed to support that. This was about more than just bikes. That's why Willie G and his partners had bought Harley back from AMF. The company had the chance to be something greater than an obscure motorcycle maker. As Mike's meeting with his hero came to an end, this much was clear to him: He belonged here. Mike took the job.

Little by little, Harley began to turn the corner. And thanks to the efforts of a lot of dedicated people who worked hard to connect with and celebrate riders, the organization suddenly began to grow at an astounding rate. Mike was now among his tribesmen, and he knew intuitively how to help Harley's business grow. He quickly rose to become a leader of the Harley-Davidson pack, heading up the Harley Owner's Group (H.O.G.), the million-member club that represents the heart and soul of the company's business.

More than a quarter-century later, Mike Keefe has become a full-time resident of two very different worlds. As he sees it, there's Juneau World, the Harley offices at 3700 Juneau Avenue where his desk resides, and there's H.O.G. World, the free land where he, his motorcycles, and his million closest friends can discover everything else there is to learn about life.

"I could sit here and basically learn nothing about what's really going on in the hearts and minds of the H.O.G. members," he says, gesturing around his cubicle, "or I could go out and see the people who matter the most."

He has such a close connection to the company's riders that when Mike walks in H.O.G. World, he's just another rider with a story to tell and dreams to live out. As he swaps stories and shares campfires with other riders, he gets bombarded with reminders of Harley's larger mission beyond next quarter's results.

Mike is the ideal person to lead the H.O.G. organization. He's both a prototypical Harley rider and a great marketing manager. He blurs the line between the company and the people it serves. Mike has an empathic connection to the riders who have made Harley-Davidson what it is today. To him, hanging out with riders and fans of Harley is the most important work he can do. Because Mike and his team blur the line between Juneau World and H.O.G. World, they help Harley stay focused on what's important to riders. And what's important to them is more than just going for a ride.

As Willie G first showed Mike back in 1984, motorcycles are a medium for personal expression and community building.

They're folk art for modern times. At its best, Harley-Davidson restores some of the tribal bonds that we've lost as a society. While the company may once again face hard times, it will succeed over the long term if it stays true to that mission. "The future of Harley-Davidson is 10,000 years ago," Mike says. "People are very neolithic. And the neolithic human within all of us still remembers the cave." That's a sense of mission that extends far beyond the bike. At the end of the day, Harley-Davidson riders aren't just the stereotypical biker gangs of movies. They're doctors, lawyers, politicians, teachers, journalists, and yes, construction workers. They're people like you and me.

Mike and other folks at Harley blur the line between producer and consumer. They work to ensure that Harley-Davidson becomes the place its riders need it to be. Empathy makes the company much more than a motorcycle manufacturer. It's a millions-strong army of riders and enthusiasts who develop the close bonds that so many people lack these days. That's what helped Harley dig itself out of the bad old days of the early 1980s—creating connections between people is perhaps the greatest growth opportunity of all.

Like anything else, though, widespread empathy requires constant attention in order to work. When organizations become more concerned with their own needs than they are with serving people out in the world, they begin to lose their advantage. Even Harley isn't immune. On the day that I most recently visited Mike Keefe at Harley-Davidson, a BMW coupe was parked across the famous motorcycle-only parking spaces at the front of company headquarters. By itself, this little infraction doesn't mean much. But if Harley doesn't defend the needs of riders, it could begin to lose its way. Widespread empathy has helped make the company what it is today. Harley will need to stay true to those values to prosper going forward. Without empathy, any great company is at risk of becoming an also-ran. With empathy, any company can stand head-and-shoulders above its peers for the long run.

HAVING FRIENDS CAN INCREASE YOUR LIFESPAN

In 2005, medical researchers in Australia studied the lifespans of the country's oldest residents. They looked at more than 1,400 men and women over the age of 70 to see what possible factors could contribute to their longevity. They considered a number of factors, including income, family size, and social interactions. To their surprise, they reached one unavoidable conclusion: People who had networks of close friends tended to lead longer lives, even longer than having strong family connections. Having friends can help you live longer.

The more we retreat into our own worlds, the less we thrive. The more we reach out, the healthier we become. Though a relatively recent medical discovery, the ability of friendship to increase our lifespans isn't a terribly surprising finding. After all, human beings wouldn't have created cities or become interested in travel unless our brains were tuned to seek out other people. It only makes sense that this same feeling of connection and belonging helps us to thrive as individuals. We're wired to care.

Having friends can increase the lifespan of companies, too. That's because when companies help other people, they really end up helping themselves. Even Henry Ford, a notoriously prejudiced individual, realized this when he decided to pay a living wage to the workers who built his Model T car. That decision helped him to create a new middle class that could afford to buy the cars they were building, which drove up sales volumes, which then allowed Ford to make the Model T even more affordable. Empathy helped Ford grow his business while also making life better for thousands of families because he was able to see that his workers could be his ideal customers. Ford saw a way to help himself by helping others.

When companies blur the line between us and them, between inside and out, opportunities appear for mutual benefit. Customers become loyal fans who evangelize the brand. Suppliers become partners who bring new ideas to the table. Even competitors become allies in helping to grow an industry. Where isolation engenders a feeling of a zero-sum game, connection suggests the possibility for widespread prosperity.

Of course, it isn't easy to blur the lines between you and the outside world. There is a host of forces that incentivize a more adversarial relationship. Especially during times of stress and adversity, it's too easy to forget what we have in common. When times get tough, the instinct of people and companies alike is to batten down the hatches and adopt a bunker mentality. When threatened, we feel safer when we isolate ourselves from others. And yet, to prosper, we need to do the opposite.

TEN

The Golden Rule

*Consistent ethical behavior demands that you
walk in other people's shoes. Because of this,
Widespread Empathy can be an effective way to
ensure the morality of a large institution, more
so than any rule book or code of conduct.*

CALIFORNIA'S SILICON VALLEY developed a very different business culture from the buttoned-down East Coast corporations that came before it. One thing that sets many Silicon Valley firms apart is that they offer their employees stock options. Stock options give employees the opportunity to buy shares in their company at a fixed price. Then, if the share price rises over the next few years, employees can exercise their options and reap the reward. In a part of the country where companies are constantly competing for talent, it's a way to incentivize employees who stick around for the long haul and help build the value of the firm. Companies in the Valley have used stock options since Intel first offered them back in the late 1960s.

For example, if you joined one of the numerous tech firms in the Bay Area, you'd likely receive the option to buy shares of your new employer's stock at whatever price it was trading at that day. Your company might offer you the option to buy 10,000 shares of its stock, which was currently trading at, say, $15 per share. Those options would vest over the course of five years, meaning that you'd actually get to purchase 2,000 shares for each year that you stayed with the company. The hope is that the company's stock price will continue to rise so that after three years as an employee, you could buy 6,000 shares for $15 each, even if their value has risen to $30 or even $100. The benefits of stock options are tremendous: Employees get a relatively low-risk way to share in the growth of their company. Companies get a way to hold on to their best talent.

But stock options aren't guaranteed to pay off. If the stock price unexpectedly tumbles down to $2 per share, your option to buy at $15 is worthless. Options are only worth something if you can buy the stock at a price lower than what you could sell it for. And that price is set by the market. Securities regulations require companies to set the price of their options according to their fair market value on the day they are issued or take an accounting charge equal to the value of any discount. Because of that, the only way to ensure that your stock options will ever be worth anything is to work hard and grow the value of the company.

At least, that's the only *legal* way. If a company chooses to manipulate the date on a stock option, they can offer it to you at a lower price. That's called backdating. Suppose your company is all set to grant you options on June 1. On May 31, however, the price of the stock shoots up from $15 to $45. The company is required to grant you the options at $45, or else take an accounting charge to make up the difference. But your company might be trying to keep you happy and instead claim that it gave you the options on May 30, back when the stock was still worth $15. Sounds great, right? The organization gets happy employees, and employees get a massive guaranteed return. No one seems to lose.

Here's the problem: Those stock options were really worth $45 a share on June 1. The fact that the company gave them to you at $15 a share means that it essentially gave you a $30 per share payment that the company needs to record in its accounts. Simply changing the date to pretend it gave them out earlier is fraud. If the company decided to come clean later, it would need to say that you were given 10,000 shares at a $30 discount, and that its profits for that quarter were actually $300,000 less than what it had previously stated. That sort of restatement doesn't usually build shareholder confidence. It's much easier to just hide the problem. And, as it turns out, a lot of companies have done just that. They backdated stock options, and then they hid what they had done. In 2006, investigators discovered that more than 130 companies, most based in Silicon Valley, had engaged in unannounced backdating without taking accounting charges for the discounts.

When regulators came down on the companies involved, virtually all of those firms had to restate their earnings for several previous years. Several senior legal and financial officers across the Valley were charged with fraud by the Securities and Exchange Commission. Greg Reyes, the CEO of San Jose network technology company Brocade, was even tried and convicted of ten counts of fraud for his role in backdating at his company.

Amid the most widespread financial scandal in the Valley's history, some companies decided to check their records to make sure they had no issues to resolve. Among them was networking giant Cisco Systems, which had routinely granted stock options as long-term incentives for its employees since its 1984 founding. Though no stories about backdating had arisen at Cisco, the company's legal team decided to make sure that there were no problems. Cisco is, after all, a company of 65,000 people. The legal team needed to find out: Had the company ever granted options at a lower price than the fair market value?

"No!" responded Cisco's stock administrators. "You're not allowed to do that." Not only had Cisco never engaged in back-dating, but the organization's leaders had preemptively banned the practice in 1994, issuing a memo with strict orders that options be priced on the date of their granting to avoid costly accounting charges. As others struggled to get a handle on how much damage backdating had done to their financials, Cisco learned that its stock managers had never even contemplated the practice.

Why was Cisco able to avoid a pitfall that brought down so many of Silicon Valley's high flyers? A narrow view of the situation might suggest that the company got lucky because someone had bothered to write a memo. But there's a larger dynamic at work here, one that suggests a powerful indirect benefit of creating Widespread Empathy. In an industry that embraces speed, and by implication, prizes overnight success, Cisco has created a culture that focuses on the long term. And central to that culture is the company's high standard of ethical behavior.

The Cisco way of doing business is in large part thanks to Chairman and CEO John Chambers. Since his installation as the company's leader in 1995, Chambers has methodically generated long-term, sustainable growth. But John Chambers is more than a good leader. Cisco benefits every single day from his focus on other people. No matter whether Chambers is dealing with a customer, an employee, or a competitor, his belief is that you should treat others the way you want to be treated yourself. This is the Golden Rule, and it's one of John Chambers's personal core values. It's also a basic principle for business that he has infused throughout Cisco since becoming CEO. He sets

an example from the top and expects that the entire organization will do what's best for customers, employees, partners, and
shareholders. Chambers has helped Cisco become one of the
key forces of the global economy by doing the right thing.

"There are very few times when I encounter difficult situations here, in which if I ask myself 'What would John do?' I don't
come out with a better answer than I would just thinking about
it for myself," says Mark Chandler, general counsel at Cisco.

The value of the Golden Rule to Cisco was clearly demonstrated a few years back. At the time, Cisco was on the verge of
acquiring a smaller firm, with Mark leading the legal effort. As it
would with any acquisition, Cisco was working its way through
due diligence. Everything about the smaller company was
splayed open to Cisco, from revenues to earnings to tax records.
Because due diligence is so invasive and time-consuming, companies perform it only when a deal is close to being reached.
That was the situation for this acquisition, too. A press release
announcing Cisco's latest deal had already been drafted, and
the announcement was set for the next business day, a Monday.
Things were going along smoothly.

And then, at the last possible minute, the smaller firm raised
a tiny red flag that it hoped wouldn't be a problem. The company
had some previously unforeseen issues related to accounting—
nothing big, they assured Cisco, just some minor issues related
to the value of its stock options. The Cisco leaders knew that
this meant they couldn't get an accurate read on the actual value
of the company they intended to acquire. Without clear figures
for historical earnings, it would be impossible to determine a
fair acquisition price. This wasn't good.

The Cisco leaders called an emergency meeting at 7 o'clock
on a Sunday morning to figure out what they should do. Everyone quickly agreed that the deal had to be put on hold until

the accounting issues could be resolved. But since Cisco was so close to finishing its due diligence, some executives wanted to go ahead and complete the two remaining interviews with the smaller firm. That way, the work would be wrapped up in case the acquisition ever became a possibility again. Chambers wanted no part of that plan.

"How would we feel if another company in the industry was performing due diligence on us and we found out that they'd gone ahead and kept doing interviews even after they'd decided that they weren't going to do the deal?" he asked. In Chambers's mind, the right way to act was with transparency, so that the other side knew what Cisco's plans were before it continued to divulge information. Continuing the process after deciding to hold off on the deal would simply be wrong. That was his challenge to his lieutenants: Think for a minute about how you would feel if you found out someone was doing this to you. Then decide whether it's the right thing to do.

After a long pause, the assembled leaders agreed that they would immediately inform their prospective acquisition that the deal was on ice. If the smaller firm wanted to wrap up the last two due diligence interviews, Cisco would do them. Otherwise, things would end as they were. "Now that sounds like a plan," Chambers said.

Cisco held all the cards in the deal. If its leaders had wanted to, they could have learned everything about the smaller firm, with no obligation to act. That would make life easier for Cisco if it ever did look at acquiring the other firm again. But that wouldn't be fair, so Cisco shared what it knew and what it planned to do. The deal was eventually cancelled, but both parties could walk away without anyone feeling mistreated.

Such forthrightness serves Cisco well, especially now that it's one of the largest companies on Earth. With operations in nearly 140 countries and annual revenues in excess of $40 billion, it's now the 2,000-pound gorilla of networking, not just two people working in a startup. If today's Cisco treated any of its customers or potential partners with anything but integrity or respect, it would look like a bully leaning on the little guy to get what it wants. Cisco doesn't view itself as an intimidating place, but that doesn't really matter. People act toward a company based on how they see it, not the way the company sees itself. As a result, Cisco works to truly understand how other people and other companies view themselves and the world.

"We make sure we see ourselves as others see us," Mark says. "We may think we're small and cuddly, but, in fact, we've grown to be quite large. And if you let arrogance creep in, that can lead to bad results."

All of this makes it increasingly important for Cisco to act as ethically as possible. Over its history, Cisco has acquired more than 125 companies. The only way to integrate that many organizations into your company without worrying other firms is to treat everyone with the respect you'd expect for yourself. John Chambers, more than anyone else, has guided Cisco through its massive expansion, and he has succeeded in that task by making the Golden Rule part of standard operating procedure. To do that, he models the right behavior. He repeatedly asks his managers how they would feel if they were on the other side of a transaction. More than anything, he encourages everyone who works for him to understand how other people view the world. After all, you can't treat someone right unless you know how they want to be treated.

As a result, Cisco has built a culture that is governed as much by values and basic ethics as it is by policies and regulations. The organization doesn't try to legislate its way to moral behavior; it rather creates an environment where ethical decisions can flourish. From the day new hires arrive at the company onward, managers remind their employees to keep the best interests of others in mind at all times. At the organizational level, this is a remarkably novel practice. Far more companies ask their employees to meet the quarterly earnings numbers at all costs. They create high-pressure environments where success requires unethical behavior or remaining silent about wrong-doing.

John Chambers has set a standard for ethical behavior at Cisco that has become deeply embedded in the fabric of the company. General Counsel Mark Chandler says that he often hears his own employees evaluate their decisions based on the Golden Rule. On every team, someone always remembers to think about the feelings of others before acting. That's the Cisco way. It's simple, and it's effective.

"Corporations can't teach ethics," Mark recently noted. "People learn that at home, through their faith, and from their friends. At a company, you create a set of standards that you want to have, and then you have a culture that allows people to be good."

RECIPROCAL ALTRUISM

When an organization becomes focused on understanding how other people prefer to be treated, everyone inside the company benefits. Muddy ethical quandaries become crystal clear. Decision making improves at all levels. The focus by Cisco on the Golden Rule creates an environment where its people can succeed by being good instead of by being cutthroat. In a sense, empathy is a necessary prerequisite for the Golden Rule. Unless you understand where someone else is coming from, you can't really put yourself in their shoes. And since policies and procedures can't envision every possible situation, relying on the Golden Rule can be a more widely useful standard.

Using the Golden Rule as the basis of an overall business philosophy is fairly novel. But in the wider world, it's as common as table manners. After all, John Chambers didn't invent the Golden Rule. The command to consider the feelings of others ahead of one's own is actually the most common religious precept in all of human culture. Scientists call this basic guide to ethical behavior "reciprocal altruism." We behave morally because we want others to behave morally toward us. That's the biological foundation of the Golden Rule. When we act altruistically toward others, others tend to act altruistically in return.

Reciprocal altruism is everywhere in human society. From Hinduism to Judaism, Confucianism to Christianity, every major school of religious and philosophical thought shares the Golden Rule. In 1893, more than 200 leaders from over 40 religions came together for a Parliament of World Religions in Chicago. The goal was to see if they shared any common ground. Those leaders, reflecting the entire spectrum of faith, signed a document to declare that the Golden Rule was the one belief all of them shared. Dubbed "The Ethic of Reciprocity," this declaration is nothing short of stunning. Usually, when leaders of that many religions and cultures get together in the same room, they can't agree on what they should order for dinner, let alone formalize their shared beliefs. And yet, on this much, everyone agreed: The human capacity to put yourself in someone else's shoes is the root basis for moral behavior. Whether you're Buddhist or Baptist, when you're in an ethically ambiguous situation, you'll make the better choice if you just follow the Golden Rule.

And, with no offense intended to the venerable spiritual thinkers who codified this credo in ancient times, the Golden Rule is less a philosophy than a natural human behavior. Any idea with that kind of traction is likely something inherent in the human brain. The phenomenon of reciprocal thinking leading to morality existed implicitly before anyone spoke it out loud. Religion and philosophy often predate science, and in this case, the idea of the Golden Rule presaged the discovery, thousands of years later, of the neurological structures that govern our emotions. The Golden Rule articulates how our brains are wired.

IDENTITIES BLUR IN OUR MINDS

The Golden Rule leads people to behave morally. But how does that really work? Donald Pfaff, head of neurobiology at The Rockefeller University, has a pretty clear idea. He argues that the Golden Rule is hard-wired into the human brain through the brain systems that govern fear and identity. To see how this works, consider the following ethical dilemma.

You're at work around lunchtime, and you open the office's communal refrigerator. You're starving, and you need to run to a meeting in 10 minutes. Scanning through the fridge, you notice two slices of pizza in a plastic bag. The bag has the initials of your coworker Jenny on it. It's not your pizza, but you're really running late. Should you eat the pizza, or should you leave it in the fridge and stay hungry?

According to Pfaff, your brain resolves this dilemma in a four-step process. First, we represent the prospective action in the central nervous system. This happens in a number of different ways. We might visualize what we're about to do in our mind, fire the neurons that would move our limbs, or even begin to imagine the sounds and smells that would result from our actions. In the case of the pizza dilemma, our brains would picture us taking the slices, putting them in the microwave, and then eating them. It's a most pleasant vision. So far, this seems like a good idea.

Second, the human brain envisions the target of our action. We imagine what would happen to the other person if we were to carry out our proposed course of action. Picture the look on Jenny's face when she opens up the fridge. Is she surprised? Angry? Indifferent? Does she even notice that the pizza is missing?

Third, our brains blur the identity of the target with our own. While we're imagining how Jenny will react to the missing pizza when she returns to the office, our brains do something fascinating: They put us in the other person's shoes. Suddenly, we become Jenny. We begin to picture ourselves opening the fridge to discover that our own pizza is missing. The question becomes, "How would this make me feel if it happened to me? Do I get upset? Do I even notice?"

The fourth step is easy: Decide what to do. When you and Jenny begin to blur together in your mind, the correct course of action becomes clear: Leave the pizza where it lies. Discovering someone eating your leftovers would make you want to yell at the perpetrator, so it's quite likely Jenny would react the same way. What's more, an office where people steal one another's lunches is a terribly unpleasant place to work. Trust gets shattered. It's better to stay hungry and remain friends with Jenny. Next time, she might even give you some of her leftover pizza—people tend to be nice to people who are nice to them, after all. That's the way reciprocal altruism works.

In Pfaff's model, it's the outcome of the third step that ultimately governs our actions. Pfaff argues that if we find the outcome distasteful when we test our ideas on ourselves, we tend not to do it. If it feels bad to us, we wouldn't wish it on anyone else. But if, however, the outcome is neutral or positive, we're likely to do it. It's a simple process that each of us repeats subconsciously hundreds of times per day. We imagine an action, think about who it will affect, and then we see how we would feel on the receiving end. And if we have a strong enough sense for the other person's way of thinking, we do the right thing.

We are far more predisposed to lapses in ethical behavior when we fail to put ourselves in other people's shoes. For most of us, those lapses are occasional. For a dangerous few, however, an inability to envision others is central to their pathology. Studies of serial killers show that they have an inability to grasp what their victims were feeling. Policemen often come home with stories of such sociopathy. One New York police officer recounted the case of a teenage mugger who was asked how he could bring himself to cripple an 83-year-old woman. Without missing a beat, the young boy looked up and replied, "What do I care? I'm not her."

Understanding the neurological basis for the Golden Rule is instructive for two reasons. First, it confirms that humans are predisposed to moral behavior. Second, it shows that moral behavior is deeply dependent on our ability to envision the people that our actions will affect. Unless we can actually picture the people who might be harmed or benefited by what we do, we cannot put ourselves in their shoes. The Golden Rule becomes impossible unless the other people involved are real to us. When we become disconnected from other people, we can't behave in a consistently moral way—we simply have nothing to calibrate our behavior by.

People struggle to follow the Golden Rule when they can't envision the folks who will be affected by their actions. That's true in individual interactions, and it's true on the scale of large corporations. The Golden Rule would not be a successful guiding light for Cisco if the organization didn't also focus on empathy for other people. Knowing exactly who the people are that might be affected by your decisions leads to more ethical choices. Instead of looking for justification for ethically murky behavior, the world starts to look a bit more black-and-white: This idea is good because it will make these people happy, and that idea is bad, because it will hurt those people.

Companies often work to legislate ethical behavior in their employees through elaborate policies and regulations. But no amount of memos or codes of honor will ever convince people to consistently act in an ethical fashion unless they understand why acting ethically matters. And that requires helping employees see who people out in the world really are. That takes empathy, which individuals have in abundance but companies often lack. As a result, many companies that try to do what's right only end up making things worse.

TELLING EMPLOYEES TO DIG THROUGH TRASH

Laying off employees is the most trying part of any manager's job. Taking away another person's livelihood never feels good, and few of those who get laid off are ever prepared to handle such a crisis. Bearing this problem in mind, Northwest Airlines decided a few years back that it would handle an impending layoff differently than it had in the past. Instead of simply cutting ties and moving on, Northwest set out to help its former employees come to grips with the realities of unemployment.

In August 2006, Northwest Airlines sent out a pamphlet called "Preparing for a Financial Setback" to several hundred customer service representatives and baggage handlers whose jobs had been eliminated as part of a union concession. Across four pages, the Northwest-written document offered helpful tips for using a company-sponsored financial planning service— and for setting up a piggy bank, cutting down on Starbucks expenses, and getting the most out of grocery store coupons. The pamphlet was not an inherently bad idea, but it needed to be written by someone who understood how getting laid off feels. You can't treat other people right if you don't have any sense for what they're going through.

Northwest's pamphlet came across as the opposite of caring or concerned. It was mostly insulting. One section, entitled "101 Ways to Save Money," is so painfully out of touch with ordinary people that it's difficult to read. The most astonishing inclusion is Tip No. 46: "Don't be shy about pulling something you like out of the trash." Wow. I can't think of a worse thing to say. "Don't worry about losing your job! There's plenty of nice stuff in the garbage that you can have for free!" That's not something that a real person would ever say to another human being—it's way too callous.

Interestingly, many of the suggestions on the "101 Ways" list, such as renegotiating a mortgage at a more favorable interest rate or buying clothes once they're out of season, are tactics that anyone could follow to better mind their money. These aren't just tips for the unemployed. But equating energy-saving tactics like switching off lights in empty rooms with dumpster diving only shows a profound lack of empathy. Northwest management understood neither the lifestyles of its employees while they were employed nor the challenges that they faced once they lost their jobs. In trying to show that it cared, Northwest accidentally demonstrated how removed its leaders were from not only its customers but its employees, as well.

When criticized for the pamphlet, Northwest struggled to apologize, not entirely certain what it had done wrong. A Northwest spokesman worked to defuse the situation. "We do realize that some of the information in there might be a bit insincere and, for that, we do apologize. There are some tips in there that are very useful, and there are some tips that, looking back, were a tad insensitive." Well, not really. Asking an employee to work a bit late on his anniversary is a tad insensitive. Telling people who you just laid off to dig through the trash is inhuman. The mistake Northwest made as a company is one that few individuals could ever make. Only by becoming part of a large organization that is disconnected from others is it possible to do something so unfeeling.

THREE LEVELS OF THE GOLDEN RULE

Like Northwest, many companies struggle to understand how they should behave toward their own employees, their customers, and the rest of the world. Most companies fully intend to behave morally. Unfortunately, without empathy, they're unable to do so because they lack any sense for how other people want to be treated. For them, the Golden Rule provides little guidance.

In a sense, the Golden Rule is actually three different rules. The first and most basic version, "Do unto others as you would have them do unto you," has limited efficacy. It's contingent on people sharing the same outlook. If we were to follow this rule to the letter, we would only end up propagating our own worldview. Consider the joke about a husband who decides to follow the Golden Rule when selecting a gift for his wife's birthday. After she blows out the candles on her birthday cake, the man urges his wife to open up her present. Tearing open the gift, his wife is shocked to discover that she has received a brand-new chainsaw. She looks up. "Oh, Honey," she says. "It's just what you've always wanted!" Knowing how *you* prefer to be treated only means that you have a good sense for how to treat other people who are a lot like you.

That's what makes Google's corporate motto so toothless. The company gained some fame for its "Don't be evil" policy. Over time, that has been a tough standard to satisfy. While the company's corporate web site cites unwanted advertising as an example of evil that it avoids, critics have taken issue with other actions. Authors have protested that Google's initiative to digitize library books robs them of their copyrights. Human rights groups have strongly condemned Google's decision to comply with the Chinese government's censorship standards. Is this evil? Well, that depends on who you are and who else you're taking into account. Merely doing as you would have done to you might not be enough. As any good actor knows, every villain is a hero in his own mind.

Acting morally toward people who have different experiences, beliefs, and histories from your own requires that you understand how *they* want to be treated. That's the second iteration of the Golden Rule: "Do unto others as they would have done to them." Through a greater amount of empathy, you can discover what's going on with other people, what they need, and how they like things to work. That's what John Chambers encourages Cisco employees to do on a daily basis.

Merely treating other people as they want to be treated doesn't inherently lead to good outcomes. A lot of people are interested in things that are bad for themselves or for society. To act in a truly ethical manner, companies need to find the common ground in how we'd all like to be treated, inside the company and out. This third version of the Golden Rule is the most complex but the most important in terms of encouraging ethical behavior: "Do unto each other as we would have done unto us."

Sports apparel maker Patagonia has always led the business community in finding ways to benefit all of society. Much of the company's clothing is made from synthetic fibers that wear and tear but fail to decompose like natural materials do. That fleece jacket in your closet will probably be around long after you're gone. In 2005, Patagonia launched Common Threads, a

garment recycling program. Customers can return worn out
clothing to Patagonia, and the company will recycle the polyester fibers into new clothing. This means fewer jackets end up
in landfills. It also means that future Patagonia products will
require less virgin polyester and, therefore, less petroleum.
Notably, the company will even take back competitors' gar-
ments. The company realizes this is a problem that's bigger than
Patagonia alone.

How is this more than just doing unto others as they would
have done to them? Polyester recycling wasn't something customers were clamoring for, but Patagonia started the program
out of a larger commitment to be a responsible resident of the
planet. When you have an empathic connection to the world
around you, you're doing more than treating people as you
want to be treated. You might even treat people better than *they*
expect to be treated. When you realize that "we are them and
they are us," the Golden Rule can be the whole of the law.

KNOWING TORTURE WHEN YOU SEE IT

The Republican candidates for president in 2008 found themselves in a moral quagmire. America was fighting not one, but
two foreign wars. The United States had a compelling interest
to discover information that could prevent terrorist attacks.
That might mean going a little further with suspects than a typical chat down at the police station. Where exactly was the line
between interrogation and torture? Was the interrogation technique known as water-boarding torture? Well, who could say
either way?

Former New York Mayor Rudy Giuliani couldn't make up
his mind. This was a very gray issue. He wouldn't be pinned
down on one side of the question or the other. "It depends on

how it's done," Giuliani told *The Washington Post.* "It depends on the circumstances. It depends on who does it."

Candidate Mitt Romney, for his part, thought it was inappropriate to even talk about the interrogation methods of the United States. "I'm not going to specify the specific means of what torture is and what is not torture so that the people that we capture will know what things we're able to do and what things we're not able to do," Romney said, concerned that the secrets of the U.S. military could be turned against America.

In an age of complex, ambiguous, and unpredictable threats, ethics aren't cut-and-dried. We can set standards for behavior, but ultimately, situations can arise when such standards should be ignored. What should you do when you've captured an enemy combatant that you believe will tell you how to save thousands of lives if you just push him far enough? Well, argued many of the Republican candidates, you might have to do what's best for the greater good, even if that included water-boarding, a form of controlled drowning. Is it really torture when you use strong interrogation techniques to save lives? Who's to say? Where is the line between right and wrong? What is torture, really?

Arizona Senator John McCain, who ultimately won the Republican nomination, had no difficulty judging the ethics of water-boarding. "All I can say is that it was used in the Spanish Inquisition, it was used in Pol Pot's genocide in Cambodia, and there are reports that it is being used against Buddhist monks today," McCain told *The New York Times.* Blasting his colleagues, he said the situation was far less gray and far less complex than other contenders made it out to be. "They should know what it is. It is not a complicated procedure. It is torture."

McCain should know. He was a prisoner of war. While serving as a Navy pilot during the Vietnam War, McCain's plane was shot down in territory controlled by the northern Vietnamese,

who took him to a prison camp. They denied him treatment for
his broken arms and legs, and then they placed him in solitary
confinement without adequate food and water. One day, his
guards beat him savagely from head to toe for hours before tying
him up with ropes and leaving him in the middle of a floor. This
continued for a week. Each day, he was beaten for two to three
hours. His left arm was broken again, and his ribs were cracked.
His captors demanded confessions to a variety of fictional
crimes against Vietnam. For five long years, McCain endured
this torture. At the same time, he saw his captured comrades
suffer greater indignities—bamboo shoots shoved under their
fingernails, cigarettes stubbed out on their chests. At one point,
McCain felt close to suicide. When he was finally released in
1973, he was no longer the lean, mean, fighting machine he had
been when he went to war. By the time he returned to the U.S.,
McCain has been so badly abused that he was incapable of rais-
ing his arms over his head.

As a result of the savage torture he experienced in Vietnam,
John McCain didn't spend too long puzzling over the moral
implications of water-boarding. The issue was clear to him. It's
torture. End of story. McCain had been a prisoner of war, and he
had tremendous empathy for other prisoners of war as a result.
He believed that no one should have to go through what he had.
It doesn't matter who, how, or why it's done, water-boarding is
torture, and torture is wrong. Everyone ought to know that. In
the chaos of a political campaign, John McCain didn't need to
imagine himself in someone else's shoes to determine right from
wrong. This time, the shoes he wore were his own.

Questions of ethics can often feel incredibly complex. Gov-
erning laws and regulations contradict each other, specific situations seem to call for different standards than the norm, and
critical objectives can overrule other considerations. Particularly

in large, multinational corporations, it can seem nearly impossible to tell right from wrong. But it doesn't have to be this way. Organizations that have real empathy for the people they serve can be governed by the simplest law of all: the Golden Rule. When you've walked in another person's shoes, you make better intuitive judgments about how a certain course of action might make them feel. And when you can create a company that offers its employees this kind of clarity and connection to the people they serve, something else happens: Work itself becomes more meaningful.

ELEVEN

The Hidden Payoff

*Having empathy for others can do more
than drive growth. It can also give people
the one thing that too many of us lack: a
reason to come in to work every day.*

EARLY IN HIS CAREER, Chip Conley had to face up to a hard truth. Chip is the passionate and charismatic founder of San Francisco's Joie de Vivre hotel group. More than creating a hotel chain, Chip had the dream of building a company that was devoted to caring for people far from home. Over time, though, he began to realize that he'd never be able to fulfill that mission if he couldn't get his employees to share in it, as well. Imbuing a sense of mission in employees is incredibly hard to do in a business with huge turnover. A typical hotel can see as many as sixty percent of its employees leave in a given year. Chip needed to find a way to retain his talent.

One way to retain employees would be to keep wages high, but that was a temporary solution. Any competitor that really wanted to could match a wage hike. Besides, Chip could raise wages only so much before the price of a night's stay became too high for the vast majority of travelers. As he relates in his memoir, *Peak*, Chip wanted to make JDV a long-term destination for the best frontline hotel crews in the country, not just another stop in the hospitality circuit. To do that, he needed to do more than provide fair compensation or a pleasant workplace. He needed to make work more meaningful.

To better understand what that might look like, Chip and his executive team decided to accompany housekeeping crews as they cleaned rooms and prepared for new guests. Shoulder-to-shoulder with housekeepers, the executive team made up beds, vacuumed floors, swapped out towels, and listened to what the housekeepers had to say. The executives soon learned that being a housekeeper was really about delivering the promise of a great stay. The housekeepers were the people who were responsible for making sure that a guest's room matched up to JDV's brand image. If their rooms weren't perfectly cleaned and made ready, travelers didn't have a good experience. If the housekeepers didn't do their jobs well, the hotel's guests wouldn't enjoy a sense of well-being or peace of mind. JDV's ability to offer its guests the "joy of life" ultimately came down to the dedication of its housekeepers. And yet, many housekeepers didn't realize how important they were.

To illustrate the power that housekeepers had, JDV executives asked them to do an experiment. For two days, they were asked to forget their standards. To not try too hard. To cut corners. The staff was asked to take it easy and watch what happened. The housekeepers took to the experiment with zest. They stopped fluffing pillows in just the right way. They didn't scrub the bathrooms until they sparkled. They didn't stack the towels immaculately. Everyone made sure to do a mediocre job.

The impact was immediate. After two days of adequate but uninspiring service, the experiment had taken its toll on the hotel's guests. Guests said "please" and "thank you" less often. They spoke curtly with the front desk when asking for service in their rooms. They left smaller tips at breakfast. They just weren't the kind of friendly, contented guests that Joie de Vivre was used to. Then the company asked guests about what it had felt like to watch the quality of service crash during their stay. All the guests agreed that while the last two days hadn't been unbearable, they were surprised by how much they missed the little touches that the housekeepers were deliberately leaving out. No one needed an expertly fluffed pillow, but they missed them when they were gone. Those little details were what made a good hotel into a great one. The housekeeping staff listened in on the feedback from the guests, and they heard again and again about how much their work really mattered.

Joie de Vivre has quickly become one of the best small hotel companies in the United States because its leaders do what they can to connect the actions of their employees to their impact on guests. Chip says that helping his employees find meaning in their work is one of his most important mandates. Workers at JDV are empowered to do great work. More important, they're presented with a clear picture of what their work does to the mood and friendliness of the hotel. Chip says that he can always tell when someone on his staff recognizes the importance of her work. "When you see that someone is energized as opposed to depleted in their eight or ten hours each day, you know that you've made the right decision. A job will deplete you, a calling will energize you, and a career is somewhere in between."

A HUMBLING CALL TO SERVICE

The housekeeping staffs at Joie de Vivre aren't alone. All of us have a more fulfilling experience when we can see the impact that our work has on other people. We all want a job that pays well, provides for our family's future, and doesn't stress us out too much. But we also crave a sense of meaning, a feeling that our work really matters. We want to be able to draw a direct line from our own actions as individuals to some larger effect in the world.

Throughout this book, you've seen how widespread empathy for the world around you can drive growth, improve decision making, and avoid painful mistakes and lapses in judgment. But empathy can do more than that. It can also provide something that many of us lack: a reason to come in to work every day. When we have an empathic connection to the people we serve, we can't help but get a tangible sense of the difference we can make. Empathy helps transform jobs into careers and careers into callings. As Chip Conley realized, any company can offer a higher salary and better benefits. That won't get workers to stick around. The organizations that people choose to spend a lifetime working for are the ones that can offer them meaning in their lives. That's the hidden payoff of creating widespread empathy. Empathy leads to growth—not only for organizations, but also for the individuals who work for them.

For many people, that firsthand experience can be humbling. It can remind them of why they got into a line of work to begin with. It can be a realization of their connection to other people. And it can be a call to service. For many, the experience of seeing the folks who are affected by their work triggers their limbic system in ways that are unexpected, creating a visceral response. Suddenly, they come to realize that they're part of something much larger than themselves. That moment of awareness can be life changing. Sometimes, it can even be world changing.

CONNECTING WITH THE COMMON MAN

When Mohandas Gandhi arrived in South Africa in 1893, he considered himself a dignified, contributing member of the British

Empire. Born in India, Gandhi had been educated in law at University College London and had come to South Africa to serve as an attorney in Pretoria. Within days of his arrival in the colony, however, Gandhi learned that his education, income, and position didn't define who he was in the eyes of South African authorities. To them, he was still an Indian and, by definition, a third-class citizen. That opinion was hammered home during his train ride to Pretoria. Gandhi insisted, quite reasonably, on sitting in the first-class seat he had paid for. The railroad's guard asked him to move to third-class with the other nonwhites. Gandhi declined and soon found himself being flung off the train.

Furious at his treatment, Gandhi vowed to win equal rights for Indians living in South Africa. They were members of the British Empire, and they deserved to be treated that way. He quickly became well known in the press as a dedicated community organizer of the South African Indian community. He wrote editorials for newspapers, conducted letter-writing campaigns and staged demonstrations. Though he was arrested on multiple occasions, he never encouraged violence, but he never backed down, either. He was a calm and articulate force for social change. By appealing to the intelligence of the English, Gandhi thought, he would be able to help all Indians secure their rights as members of the empire. Of course, if Gandhi had stopped there, most of us in the West might never have heard of him. It was only after he actually spent time with the poor and downtrodden of his homeland that he discovered his true mission.

In 1901, Gandhi traveled by steamship to Calcutta to attend a congress of politicians who sought to win India's independence from British rule. He had become a leader of Indians abroad, and the trip to Calcutta was his chance to lead Indians in India. Gandhi wanted the gathered Indian National Congress to pass a resolution condemning the South African's government's discriminatory actions against Indians. In his mind, the bill represented everything that he had fought for in South Africa. The bill passed easily, but his triumph was bittersweet.

The longer that Gandhi spent time with the other members of the Congress, the less optimistic he felt. Looking around the hall, he saw nothing but wealthy Indian men dressed in expensive English suits, smoking fine cigarettes. Many had received British educations and had British-style aspirations. These were India's elite. For them, oppression was more of an abstract idea than a tangible experience. They were used to being waited on hand and foot. Indeed, Gandhi watched as the elites sat idly by, complaining when the servants at the hall found themselves unable to keep pace with the size of the Congress. Gandhi shocked the other attendees by actually picking up a broom and helping with the sweeping. To the horror of his peers, he even cleaned the toilets.

With this act, Gandhi realized that what he had been fighting for over the previous eight years of his life had been a mirage. He had dedicated his life to fighting for the rights of Indians, only to discover that he didn't know the first thing about them. All he knew of India were the aristocrats whose company he now shared. This much was clear: Removing the British would do little to improve life for the man on the street if independence put India in the hands of another elite class.

In search of a new path, Gandhi left Calcutta for Poona, a city near Bombay that was home to Gopal Krishna Gokhale, an influential figure in the independence movement. Unlike other political thinkers in India, Gokhale had not been born into wealth. Instead, he had risen from a commoner's background to become a respected academic and public intellectual. The two men talked for days about the land of their birth and the people in it. Gokhale told Gandhi that if he really wanted to understand India, he would need to leave the corridors of power and walk with the common man. Gandhi needed to get on a train and see India as it really was—not as he imagined it to be. Taking Gokhale's advice to heart, Gandhi purchased a train ticket and set off on the most important journey of his life. This time, he made sure to travel third class.

As the Indian landscape raced by, Gandhi became intimately acquainted with what life was like for his countrymen. He was packed into overstuffed railcars that were too full for him to breathe. He rode atop the train with the poorest riders, feeling the wind rush by as they baked beneath a burning sun. He spent time in villages, where he saw farmers dying of starvation and lacking the money to pay their landlords because the British had forced them to farm only cash crops. He saw children and families without shelter of any kind, living in filth. He saw communities that had been systematically split into tightly held enclaves that were suspicious of one another: Muslims against Hindus, northerners against southerners. More than anything, he saw a mighty people who had been literally divided and conquered by a foreign power. Gandhi recognized why he had been so uncomfortable at the Indian National Congress: Those men in suits did not truly represent India. They reflected the outlook of the English aristocracy. If they were to lead India, the country would remain as divided as it already was.

When Gandhi started out in South Africa, he had just wanted to ride a train in the seat he had paid for. His work as an activist had expanded his thinking, and he had then fought for his rights as a British subject. Now, meeting his countrymen for the first time, Gandhi realized he had a larger calling. Before his journey on India's railways, Gandhi had more in common with the educated elites than he did with the nation's poor. But firsthand contact had created a deep connection with ordinary people. And it revealed the magnitude of their need. For Gandhi, it was a humbling call to service. Trying to lead India while dressed like an Englishman would do nothing to change the nation.

So Gandhi took off his suit and began to dress like the Indians he met. He wore a dhoti, a single piece of cloth wrapped about his legs and knotted at the waist, and a shawl made of homespun cloth. Although he began his journey as a community organizer of considerable reputation, Gandhi transformed himself into a common man of India. He realized that British imports were keeping Indians beholden to a foreign power, and he began to encourage other Indians to buy and use only local goods, from crops to dry goods to sea salt. To win political independence from the British, he argued, the people first needed to become economically self-reliant. Paradoxically, Gandhi became the father of a country by becoming its most humble figure. The young man who wanted to legislate change with his rich friends grew into an old man who changed the world by living like the poorest of his countrymen.

FINDING THE PROFOUND IN THE PROSAIC

It might be a little grandiose for most of us to compare our own careers to Gandhi's. Few of us get out of bed in the morning thinking we're going to start a revolution, much less become the spiritual leader of a nation. That said, it is possible for each of us to experience a call to service that's every bit as profound as what Gandhi felt when he was riding the trains with the common man. That call comes when we see the impact of our work. Most of us have an impact on more people than we realize. Early on in this book, I talked about how the Industrial Revolution created a rift between producers and consumers. It's important to remember that the Industrial Revolution was also a good thing, not only for the prosperity it created, but also because it allowed us to have a global impact on other people.

In my time working with large companies, I've never come across a category of product or service that didn't have the potential to make someone's life significantly better. And I haven't always worked with hospitals and schools. Most of my experience is with things like snack foods, engineering thermoplastics, and financial services. In every case, there were people whose lives were deeply affected by the work my client did. Within the prosaic activities of daily business hid the potential to have a profound impact on other people. That isn't to say that this impact was always easy to see. It usually wasn't. More troubling, though, has been the number of people within those organizations who were resigned to the belief that they didn't have much of an impact on the world, either as an individual or as an organization.

Perhaps one of the most depressing bits of jargon in Corporate America is the idea of the Low-Interest Category. More than a few business leaders seem perfectly willing to declare that no one cares about their products, and that's okay. According to these people, there's a whole mess of junk in the world that we make for no reason except that it somehow makes money. Customers, for their part, supposedly purchase this same junk for no other reason than that their spouses happened to write it on the grocery list. People will buy it regardless, so there's no point in trying to make it better. This is the same kind of thinking that led the coffee companies to replace their high-quality roasts with cheaper Robusta blends. Products that are viewed as low-interest categories often struggle to command any sort of price premium. They're almost impossible to differentiate. And the companies that make them are often unable to grow.

Despite the idea's prevalence, low-interest categories are a myth. People don't spend money without good reason. They might not pay much attention to what they buy, but that may have more to do with what's available than what's possible. Low-interest categories are indicators of a lack of interest on the part of the companies that make them. When companies create an empathic connection to the people who use a product, high interest miraculously appears. And the impact can be profound.

CLEANING IS AN ACT OF CARE

The scene opens in a comfortable, middle-class living room in a town outside of Chicago. Seated around the coffee table are John and Christie, a married couple in their late 30s, and their teenage sons Brian and Shaun. The interviewer has been asking the family about how chores get done around the house, and the conversation is starting to get uncomfortable. Looking at her family, Christie insists that they see how all of them need to take care of their home. "We all help dirty it up," she says, "so we should all help clean it up." As Shaun rolls his eyes, Brian, the elder son, starts to snicker. Christie is clearly frustrated. "I'm glad I can entertain you," she says dryly. She turns to the interviewer apologetically and explains, "We're not used to being in this close proximity. Unless we're eating, we're all off in our own separate rooms.... I guess we don't like each other that much." John starts to protest but ultimately offers no reply.

The interviewer moves on to ask about which subjects the family can agree upon. They look at each other, laugh uncomfortably, and struggle to come up with something. Going on vacation? Money? Finally, John offers up an example. "One thing we all agree on...well, not so much you," he says, nodding at Christie as she turns away, "but the three of us all like football."

John turns to each of his sons, "You like football? You like football?" The boys smile and nod. John shrugs. "Mom tolerates it." Christie tries to engage her sons, reminding them that they also like shopping. But it's too late. She's already been cut out of the conversation. Brian turns to his dad. "Well, just the cool people in this family like football." Christie turns away from her boys and starts to fiddle with a bowl on the coffee table. Though she shares a couch with her sons, they might as well be sitting in different rooms.

As the video clip came to an end, I turned back to the audience. Seated around the conference room were twenty-five marketers and product developers from the Clorox Company. Jump had been working with Clorox for several months on a project to improve bathroom cleaning, a supposedly low-interest category. Now, in the final project presentation, we had presented a portfolio of new product concepts, ranging from things like disposable toilet wands to whole new businesses that Clorox could start. The team had responded favorably to the ideas, which meant that it was time to shift the conversation to discuss a much larger opportunity for the company.

The video of Christie, John and their sons had been uncomfortable to watch. The boys were cruel to their mother, and Dad did nothing to help matters. The scene was depressing. Heartbreakingly, it also wasn't out of the ordinary. Christie wasn't the only mom out there who felt unappreciated and disconnected from her family. Issues like these exist in homes all across America. I had shown the clip because Clorox had the power to do something about it.

We all know that moms traditionally do most of the housework. For Christie and millions of women like her, cleaning the bathtub is one act in a litany of tasks that they perform for their loved ones. Some of these things, like baking cookies, are appreciated and valued by their families. Others, like cleaning the bathroom, aren't. For millions of moms, cleaning is an act of love, but that love usually goes unrequited. Baking cookies can make Mom a hero. Cleaning a toilet just makes her a janitor. Every day, women across the country get up in the morning and clean their homes to help out their families. And every day, many of them are told that they're stupid or lacking in ambition or just uncool for taking care of their families. They spend the bulk of their productive lives caring for others in ways that no one seems to value—not even the people that they care for. Clorox had to do something to change this situation.

When we think about widespread problems with tragic consequences, our minds go to big killers like AIDS, cancer, and war. Making it easier to be a mom, by contrast, can seem like a smaller mission. But it really isn't. It's about soothing the thousand little deaths that each of us feels every day. Some people have become so used to being taken for granted, so ignored by their own families, that their pain gets swept under the rug, where it builds up over time. That's the sort of nagging, chronic pain that can make a woman wake up one day, divorce her husband, leave her family, and move across the country to start a new career. And it's the kind of pain that Clorox had the opportunity to help alleviate. Moms like Christie didn't need a new lemon scent. They just needed a little acknowledgment. They needed to know that someone, somewhere cares.

Jump outlined a strategy for how Clorox could care for the caregivers. We showed them how to create brand messages that empathized with what moms go through. We also showed them how to create products that not only cleaned the bathroom, but turned Mom into a hero. As I wrapped up the presentation, I reiterated how the strategy would be good for Clorox's business, how it would differentiate the company in the marketplace, and how it fit with Clorox's existing brand. Finally, I noted that there was one overriding reason why all of this was a good idea. Over the previous few months, I had spent a lot of time with Clorox employees. And they were all too decent, too smart, and too talented to spend the rest of their lives hawking bleach. They had the opportunity to do something more important in this world, and they owed it to themselves to seize it.

And just then, something unexpected started to happen. The room fell silent. A few folks looked around nervously at each other. And a few of them started to cry. You see, the video of Christie represented more than a promising business opportunity. It represented a reason to come into work every day. For people who had spent years hammering away at what they had been told was a low-interest category, the video offered a chance for professional transformation. It showed them why their work mattered and what they could do to make things better.

After the presentation, an executive from Clorox came up to me and said, "I want to be part of the company you described, but that isn't the company I work for. And I don't know how to turn it into that." And she was right. Transforming a huge company wouldn't happen overnight. For starters, Clorox needed to stop doing things that actively insulted moms. At the time, the company sponsored a weeklong series of James Bond movies on TNN that was called "Bleached Blonde Bimbos Week—Sponsored by Clorox!" It's obnoxious for any company to cater to male chauvinism, but it's particularly unwise to insult the people who buy your products and pay your salary and fund your 401(k) plan. Intuitively, anyone at Clorox could understand this. Getting the company to focus on caring for mothers not only constituted a growth opportunity for the company; it had the potential to make a lot of lives better, too.

Although it has taken a few years, Clorox has started working to make the lives of moms more fulfilling and rewarding. Turning the mirror on itself, the company has launched Green Works, a line of highly effective but natural cleaning products made from substances such as coconut oil, lemon juice, and corn alcohol. Moms can trust that Green Works will keep their homes clean while also making sure not to expose their kids to noxious chemicals. Green Works considers the whole perspective of caring for a family, from hygiene to personal health. Most important, managers, chemists, packaging designers, and marketers at Clorox now have a clear picture of who they really work for. Clorox is an organization that's working hard to care for the moms who work hard to care for their families.

A WIDESPREAD SENSE OF MISSION

When executives at Clorox saw the impact that their cleaning products could have on millions of mothers across the country, a few of them were moved to tears. Housekeepers at Joie de Vivre hotels were energized by seeing how critical a well-kept room is to travelers. Everyone wants a job that matters; getting that wish, however, often turns out to be more than anyone bargained for. When faced with the impact that they can create, people realize that their rules for what makes a job good—how long the hours should be, how much vacation time is offered, what the salary looks like—are actually far less important than discovering who the people are that need them to do great work. That's true in business, it's true in politics, it's true in education, and it's even true in broad social movements.

For many of the people in this book, empathy for the outside world has translated into a renewed sense of purpose. What often started as a personal desire grew steadily into a call to service.

Nina Planck went looking for fresh vegetables and helped revitalize family farms in the process. Seamus Blackley started writing video games and ended up trying to create a canvas for a new generation of digital artists. Dave Schenone wanted to design running shoes, only to become fascinated by the young athletes who wear them. Mike Keefe thought it would be cool to have a Harley-Davidson business card with his name on it, but decades later, he and his compatriots at Harley have become the stewards of a cultural movement. In every case, a firsthand exposure to real people did more than reveal business opportunities. It provided a humbling call to service.

Throughout the course of this book, I've shared the stories of a few of the most inspired and optimistic people that I've had the privilege to meet and work with. One thing unites them: All of them felt that they were part of something larger than themselves. All of them were energized to make real changes and tangible improvements in the lives of other people. Collectively, their accomplishments are mighty. They've helped improve the diets and health of millions. They've worked to give a sense of passion and accomplishment to young athletes. They've labored to make the latter years of our lives into some of the best years of our lives. They have even helped build a sense of community and belonging that spans the globe. In every case, their work has had a positive impact on the world because they actively chose to make it so.

We've seen how empathy can be a driving force to develop more prosperous, more ethical, and more enduring companies. But it also has the power to help us see how we can change the world for the better. Ultimately, every single one of us is biologically wired to care. Scaling that ability to the level of an organization can transform its mission. When we develop real empathy for the people we serve, our jobs start to become callings. There are no low-interest problems—only problem-solvers who don't have strong connections to the people they serve. Companies can serve a higher purpose than just making money. They can create wealth by enriching the wider society we all live in. Empathy can awaken us to the power that we have to change the course of everyday life. But only if we're willing to step outside of our own preconceptions and see the world through other people's eyes.

Acknowledgments

Wired to Care is not a memoir. Still, many of the ideas in this book developed gradually in my mind over the last twenty years, so writing it has evoked a great number of flashbacks and recollections, starting, of course, with that day in college when I first sat in a wheelchair. I should therefore start out by giving thanks to my friend Muffy Davis and also to my professors Rolf Faste and Sara Little Turnbull. Thought leaders of design in their own right, Rolf and Sara once taught the Needfinding class that I now do, and it was they who first admonished me to step outside of myself and walk in other people's shoes. Years later, when I was reflecting on corporations' inability to feel what humans feel, it was Rolf who provided me with the analogy of a creature who lacked a limbic system. Rolf has since passed on and Sara has moved away, but I think of them often and hunger for want of their mentorship, their inspiration, and the occasional well-deserved smackdown.

The impetus for thinking about empathy as a widespread phenomenon came from my friend and client Ralph Jerome. Almost a decade ago, Ralph invited me to speak to a group of food scientists and chemists at Mars Corporation about customer-driven innovation. I struggled to find a way to make my thoughts on customers relevant to folks who felt their job was more about molecules than it was about people. It was in thinking about this challenge that the idea of Open Empathy Organizations was born.

This entire project would not have been worth undertaking if it hadn't allowed me to see the world through the eyes of other people. I therefore give thanks to the many inspiring folks whose stories I had the privilege to tell, from entrepreneurs like Nina Planck to heroes like Pattie Moore, from new friends like Chip Conley, Mark Chandler, Seamus Blackley, Gina Beebe and Zildjian's John DeChristopher and Jason LaChapelle to long-time friends like Mike Keefe and Dave Schenone.

A smart consultant learns a great amount from his clients. I therefore have to thank Christine Albertini, formerly of Steelcase; Beth Comstock of GE; Mary Jo Cook, Jo Henshall, Ellen Moyer, and Suzanne Sengelmann of Clorox; Erik Larsen of Mercedes-Benz; Sam Lucente of HP; Heidi Emanuel, Trisha Pergande, and all our friends at General Mills; Ray Riley of Microsoft; and Robyn Waters, Patrick Douglas, and John Morioka of Target, among many others. On a daily basis, they increase my optimism that things can and will be different in the business world. I would particularly like to thank the participants of the Jump Offsite, our annual gathering for innovation leaders, who, in forms small and large, validated for me that empathy was, indeed, an important idea and encouraged me for years to write this book.

I am firmly of the belief that the only way to develop great ideas is to immerse yourself in a community of thinkers that is smarter than you, challenges your ideas, and helps you to think better. For this reason, I am grateful for everyone at Jump. If the ideas in *Wired to Care* are any good, it's because whenever I brought the kernel of an idea into the office, twenty different Jumpsters would take that idea and beat it into shape before letting me share it with the rest of the world.

Many passionate, dedicated folks lent a hand in making sure that the content of this book was all that it needed to be, and I owe each of them a debt of gratitude. Their enthusiasm alone was sustaining during the often-draining writing process. Naushad Forbes, my long-time friend and mentor, is, without a doubt, the smartest person I've ever had the pleasure of knowing personally, and his comments provided a needed international perspective. Lara Lee provided thoughtful, pointed, and close edits to the entire document, pushing me to really think about which stories to leave in and which to take out. Ewan Morrison's dogged efforts to connect us with Cisco and make sure we got the facts just right across multiple revisions were invaluable. Kimra McPherson brought an editor's eye to the manuscript, and her demands for clarity and specificity ensured that I had more to offer than a quick song and dance. Christopher Meyer's edits and suggestions helped me to remember both the big picture and the details. Rekha Ramesh offered to read a few paragraphs and was so interested that she read the entire book and offered insightful suggestions for improvement. Clynton Taylor offered edits and comments at many steps in the process, but I'm most grateful for his ideas on how this book might be received in the world—he is the guru of guerilla marketing. Conrad Wai sat by my side and helped me edit the entire book page by page late into the night for the simple reason that it needed to be done. Lauren Pollak was one of my earliest collaborators on the ideas in this book, and it was she who helped me to develop the idea of Open Empathy

Organizations. An early draft of an article she wrote years ago set the foundation for Chapter Seven and, in turn, this book.

Others shaped the book in subtle, but no less important ways, and I am grateful to them as well. Alonzo Canada is one of the most widely read people I know and continues to feed my brain with ideas and challenge my assumptions. My long-time friend and partner Neal Moore provided great insight and thoughtfulness on how to frame this book—and more than a few much-needed laughs. My sister Nandita Patnaik provided me with continued support and guidance. Margeaux Bucher, my assistant, created the space for this book to be written by clearing my calendar and making sure I stayed focused; she attended to everything from ideas for the book's content to my personal hunger. Ann Liu and Colleen Murray helped shape the visual direction of the book you hold in your hands. Sarah Singer-Nourie's continued coaching and guidance were critical to the success of this project. My daughter, Maya, has provided me with special insight, providing an ongoing lesson in empathy like only one's child can.

I am grateful for the hard-working team at Pearson Education who are making this book a reality: Tim Moore, Lori Lyons, Kim Scott, Amy Neidlinger, Megan Colvin and, most of all, my dear friend and editor Martha Cooley, without whom I would not have written the book that has been rattling inside my brain for so many years.

Of all the folks who have played key roles in this book, three people deserve special mention and thanks. My brother Udaya Patnaik stood by me and gave the most detailed comments of any reader as I went through draft after draft on the long road to publication. He provided moral support in the darkest times and argued with me to make sure I got it right. He held me, and this book, to a higher standard.

My wife, Amanda Moran, carried me throughout the writing of this book. She held our family together even when the writing process caused me to disappear for days at a time. Amanda is a gifted and perceptive editor in her own right, and I am grateful for both her comments and her love.

Finally, I must thank Peter Mortensen, my co-author and the yin to my authorial yang, without whom this book simply would not exist. Peter began by aiding me in the search for a ghostwriter and then surprised me by wondering aloud why he was not being considered for the position. Peter has a subtlety of mind and a sharpness of wit that made the writing process a joy even in the darkest of times. He was incredibly accommodating and deft at drawing out the random stories that lay entangled in the cobwebs of my mind. He is also the quickest and most prolific son of a gun I have ever seen.

This book has been a continuing journey of discovery for me and my teammates, and, while I may no doubt look back in years to come and laugh at the limitations of the ideas presented here, right now I have reason for both celebration and acknowledgment. Thank you to all.

Endnotes

CHAPTER 1: INTRODUCTION

Page 3—We spoke with Pattie Moore by phone on April 8, 2008. Although it has been three decades since her experiment in aging, she recalls the details with astounding clarity.

Page 3—To see Pattie's transformation, seek out the video titled "Patricia Moore, Journey into Time" on YouTube. This excerpt from a 1985 documentary films several steps in the process that turned her from a twenty-something into an octogenarian. It also captures her walks around New York City.

Page 4—Pattie tells her own story in the book *Disguised*, which she co-authored with Charles Paul Conn in 1985. W Pub Group released the book, which is sadly out of print.

Page 9—We last visited Harley-Davidson headquarters on Leap Day, February 29, 2008.

Page 10—Harley-Davidson's history and performance numbers are drawn from published earnings records of the last several years, as well as from *More Than a Motorcycle,* former Harley CEO Rich Teerlink's delightful memoir, published in 2000 by Harvard Business School Press. A table on page 256 shows the company's astounding progress from 1982 to 1999.

Page 12—We met Gina Beebe at an event in southern California in December 2007.

Page 13—Dale Carnegie's *How to Win Friends and Influence People* is permanently on my shelf. He had such an important insight that it's hard to believe so many others have forgotten this book.

Page 15—Dean Takahashi's *Opening the Xbox,* published by Prima in 2002, is the definitive text on Microsoft's push into the console game market. Takahashi tells the tale better and in far more detail than we could fit into this book.

Page 16—*Halo* sales figures come from a Bungie Studios press release dated November 9, 2005.

Page 16—Xbox 360 sales figures come from a *EuroGamer* report of April 25, 2008. PS3 sales figures come from a *United Press International* report of April 21, 2008.

Page 16—Xbox earnings and revenue were calculated based on Microsoft's third-quarter 2008 earnings call, issued April 24, 2008.

Page 16—Brier Dudley of the *Seattle Times* was the first person to report that much of the Xbox team would work on the Zune, then code-named Argo. His article from July 10, 2006, does a great job describing how Microsoft hoped the device would work.

Page 17—The "airbag" comment about the Zune comes from a November 24, 2006, product review by Andy Ihnatko of the *Chicago Sun-Times*. Andy is a well-known Apple booster, so his comments should be taken with a grain of salt (most of the time) when it comes to Microsoft products.

Page 17—Zune sales figures come from a May 6, 2008, Associated Press article by Jessica Mintz entitled "Microsoft, Chasing Apple, Adds TV Shows to Zune Marketplace." Microsoft spokesman Jason Reindorp noted that Apple had sold "just north of 2 million" Zunes since launch in November 2006. Interestingly, the company had sold 1.2 million by June 2007, which suggests that Zune sales slowed between 2007 and 2008.

Page 17—The iPod sales figures were culled from eight years of Apple earnings reports, which Charles Gaba of the web site System Shootouts cataloged, charted, and graphed.

CHAPTER 2: THE MAP IS NOT THE TERRITORY

Page 19—Ken Garland chronicles, in vivid pictorial detail, the creation of the London Underground Diagram in *Mr. Beck's Underground Map,* published by Capital Transport of Middlesex in 1994.

Page 19—The history of the British Railroad is elegantly related in Oliver Green's *The London Underground—An Illustrated History,* published in 1990 by Ian Allan and now out of print.

Page 21—The definitive work by Alfred Korzybski is *Science and Sanity: An Introduction to Non-Aristotelian Systems and General Semantics,* originally published in 1933 by his own Institute of General Semantics. It's still in print, well over 900 pages long, and includes "A Non-Aristotelian System and Its Necessity for Rigour in Mathematics and Physics," the paper in which he coined "The map is not the territory."

Page 24—*Uncommon Grounds,* Mark Pendergrast's 1999 history of coffee from Basic Books, is an amazing read and an indispensable examination of our planet. He discusses the rise of Robusta in Chapter 14.

Page 25—Louis Freedberg of the *San Francisco Chronicle* writes about the demise of good coffee in his August 5, 2001, article "Coffee: Brewing a Cheaper Cup." He includes this damning quote from a Hills Bros. sales representative: "A little bit won't hurt anybody."

Page 29—IBM's remarkable turnaround is captured in Lou Gerstner's 2002 Harper Business memoir, *Who Says Elephants Can't Dance? Leading a Great Enterprise through Dramatic Change.* As a former intern from IBM's pre-Gerstner days and a long-time ThinkPad user, I can't express my admiration for him emphatically enough. His two direct quotes both come from page 61 of the paperback edition.

Page 36—The Joe Rohde story was reported by Marc Gunther and Joe McGowan in their April 1998, *Fortune* article "Disney's Call of the Wild."

Page 37—Disney's Animal Kingdom park attendance was reported in the *Orlando Sentinel* on April 4, 2007, under the headline "Disney's Animal Kingdom Sees Big Attendance Boost."

Page 39—The Delta story is drawn from personal experience talking with the company. A former executive there reconfirmed my memories.

CHAPTER 3: THE WAY THINGS USED TO BE

Page 45—The vast majority of the economic history presented here, from the change in the world productivity curve to the population acceleration, from exports to literacy, is drawn from *A Farewell to Alms—A Brief Economic History of the World,* by Gregory Clark, published in 2007 by Princeton Press. It's a magnificent accomplishment, and it actually lives up to its subtitle, which is no small feat.

Page 47—Figures for U.S. net imports and exports come from the Census Bureau report "U.S. Trade in Goods and Services—Balance of Payments Basis," released March 11, 2008, and accurate through 2007.

Page 47—The story of the off-shoring of the Tubbs Snowshoe Company was drawn from Michael Kranish's February 18, 2005, *International Herald Tribune* article: "On a Boat Going to China: Vermont Snowshoe Jobs." Jason Koornick chronicled Ed Kiniry's shift from wooden snowshoe production in a 2002 issue of *Business People Vermont.*

Page 50—We visited the headquarters of the Avedis Zildjian Co. in Norwell, Massachusetts, on March 28, 2008, where the remarkably gracious Jason LaChappelle, John DeChristoper, and Debbie Zildjian gave us more of their time than anyone really should. The back story of the company is drawn from interviews and company collateral. We have an epic account, full of stories and quotes from Jason, John, and Debbie, but we had to pull it out for use on the book's web site. It's all there, including John's amazing day shopping for shoes with Charlie Watts, the drummer of the Rolling Stones.

Page 58—We met with Nina Planck at a very noisy restaurant in New York on January 24, 2008. We shared two hours of great wine, good local food, and scintillating conversation. Nina and I first crossed paths at an internal conference for a foods company that Jump was doing some work with. There she first talked about what happens when producers confront their consumers.

CHAPTER 4: THE POWER OF AFFINITY

Page 69—Seamus Blackley's quote is drawn from page 9 of Takahashi's *Opening the Xbox,* as are many of the anecdotes about his experience before joining Microsoft. The Electronics Arts acquisition of DreamWorks Interactive is sourced from a press release EA issued on February 24, 2000.

Page 69—We also spoke with a former manager from the Xbox division to confirm the storyline and glean additional insights about the project's success.

Page 72—The study on our predisposition to identify more closely with people we think are similar to us was covered in *Scientific American* on March 19, 2008, by Nikhil Swaminathan under the headline "Politically Correct: Why Great (and Not So Great) Minds Think Alike."

Page 73—Alex Markels told the story of "It's the Economy, Stupid" once again in the pages of *U.S. News and World Report* in his January 18, 2008, article "16 Years Later, It's the Economy Again."

Page 74—James Carville writes about his upbringing and the city of Carville in the first chapter of his truculent progressive political handbook *We're Right, They're Wrong,* which Random House published in 1996.

Page 76—David Maraniss chronicled Bill Clinton's rough-and-tumble past in his 1996 biography *First in His Class,* from Simon & Schuster. It's also supplemented with information from Clinton's official biography at www.whitehouse.gov.

Page 77—The story of Bush and the grocery scanner was refuted once and for all in the *Washington Post* article "The Story That Just Won't Check Out," from February 19, 1992, by Howard Kurtz. It's a classic example of a falsehood that, once disproven, actually makes the subject look even worse.

Page 81—The Associated Press reported on the incredible drops in the Big Three's U.S. auto market share in "U.S. Automakers Market Share Lowest Ever," published August 1, 2007.

Page 83—The Associated Press reported Ford's ban on parking at a Dearborn plant on January 27, 2006. MSNBC, among other sources, retains the report in its online archives.

CHAPTER 5: WALKING IN SOMEONE ELSE'S SHOES

Page 93—Information on motor neurons was drawn from Lauralee Sherwood's *Human Physiology: From Cells to Systems,* 4th edition, published in 2001 by Brooks/Cole.

Page 93—Information on the premotor cortex was drawn from the 1998 *Electroencephalography and Clinical Neurophysiology* article "The Organization of the Cortical Motor System: New Concepts," by G. Rizzolatti, G. Luppino, and M. Matelli of the Universita di Parma, Italy.

Page 94—Mirror neurons are discussed at length in a wonderful article by David Dobbs entitled "A Revealing Reflection," from the April/May 2006 issue of *Scientific American Mind.*

Page 94—Even better is *Mirroring People: The New Science of How We Connect with Others* by Marco Iacoboni, published in 2008 by Farrar, Straus and Giroux. Iacoboni is a neuroscientist based at UCLA.

Page 96—ESPN's David Whitley wrote a comprehensive article on Lawrence Taylor to accompany the channel's *SportsCentury* special on LT. Entitled "L.T. was Reckless, Magnificent," the piece can still be read at ESPN.com. Many of the concrete facts of his career, both good and bad, were drawn from here. Other stats were drawn from his page at NFL.com, which hosts official stats.

Page 96—We confirmed the date of the game that ended Joe Theismann's career via the NFL's official stats at NFL.com.

Page 97—The *New York Times* covered Joe Theismann's MVP win for the 1983 season in its December 21, 1983, issue.

Page 98—Footage of the actual hit, and the quote from Carl Banks, comes from *ESPN SportsCentury: Lawrence Taylor,* which originally aired on September 14, 2000.

Page 98—Lawrence Taylor talked about his unwillingness to watch the hit on Theismann during a January 2007, interview on HDNet's *Face 2 Face with Roy Firestone.*

Page 99—We interviewed Dave Schenone of Nike in San Mateo, California, on November 9, 2007. It was a fantastic conversation, and we regret only that we found no way to work in his story about the time he hospitalized four of his competitors during a triathlon.

CHAPTER 6: EMPATHY THAT LASTS

Page 110—Brad Lewis's adventures as an assistant cook in the French Laundry were immortalized in Kim Severson's *New York Times* article "A Rat with a Whisk and a Dream," published June 13, 2007. The film's production notes provide far more detail on the subject.

Page 112—To learn more about the relationship between emotion and our neurology, we highly recommend *A General Theory of Love,* by psychiatrists Thomas Lewis, Fari Amini, and Richard Lannon. They discuss the limbic system at length in pages 22–31, and their interpretations of its meaning fill the rest of the book. It was published in 2000 by Random House.

Page 113—The relative size of the neocortex was drawn from "Co-Evolution of Neocortex Size, Group Size, and Language in Humans," by R. I. M. Dunbar of the Department of Anthropology at University College London. One fascinating detail Dunbar notes is that the larger our neocortex has become, the larger our social groups have become. His article originally ran in *Behavioral and Brain Sciences* in 1993.

Page 114—Information on the interplay between the amygdala and the hippocampus that leads us to form more vivid memories comes from Dr. Elizabeth A. Phelps's April 2004 *Current Opinion in Neurobiology* article "Human Emotion and Memory: Interactions of the Amygdale and Hippocampal Complex." A dry title, but an informative article.

Page 120—Lou Gerstner writes about Operation Bear Hug on pages 49 and 50 of his memoir.

CHAPTER 7: OPEN ALL THE WINDOWS

Page 125—Lucien Rhodes and Patricia Amend first reported the story of Jack Stack and SRC in *Inc.* magazine in August 1986. Their article, "The Turnaround: How a Dying Division of International Harvester Became One of America's Most Competitive Small Companies," on pages 42–48, is still a classic.

Page 126—Details of open-book management are detailed in "Springfield ReManufacturing Bought the Company and Learned to Play the Game of Open-Book Management," a December 22, 1993, article in *National Productivity Review.*

Page 127—*Inc.*'s cover story on open-book management appeared in June 1995, under the headline "The Open-Book Revolution." John Case's piece of the same name is essential reading.

Page 130—Henry Mintzberg's ice-cold condemnation of traditional strategic planning comes on page 321 of his classic *The Rise and Fall of Strategic Planning,* published in 1994 by Free Press. Much of the discussion of the performance of companies dedicated to strategic planning in the 1960s and '70s is derived from his third chapter, "Evidence on Planning," from pages 91 to 158 in the first hardcover edition.

Page 131—The Environmental Protection Agency discusses Sick Building Syndrome in depth on its web site about internal air quality. The content we studied was published under the name "Indoor Air Facts No. 4 (Revised) Sick Building Syndrome."

Page 133—I know about the Target store at Target headquarters because I have shopped there. Target has been a Jump client for many years.

Page 134—Target's change of dress code was noted by *Minneapolis/St. Paul Business Journal* senior reporter Mark Reilly, who wrote the article "Clothiers Cash In on Target Dress Code" on September 17, 2004. Even then, it was evident that Target was driving business to other stores.

Page 134—Ryan Blistein wrote about the perks at Netflix for the *Oakland Tribune* in his March 22, 2007, article "Vacation Policy at Netflix: Take As Much As You Want." He discusses the free membership and DVD player, which employees earn after three months on the job.

Page 135— I have known Tony Salvador of Intel for many years.

Page 136—Basketball hoops are everywhere at Spalding. It helps that the company is practically next door to the Basketball Hall of Fame.

Page 137—Smith & Hawken discusses its company garden at the company's press web site in the Background section.

Page 138—This story of Nike is drawn from my own experiences.

CHAPTER 8: REFRAME HOW YOU SEE THE WORLD

Page 150—Target's back-to-school performance was copresented by Target design director Patrick Douglas and myself at a 2004 conference. Growth rates for 2007 were drawn from "Strong

Retail Sales Allay Holiday Worries," by James Covert of *The Wall Street Journal,* published September 7, 2007.

Page 157—Dave Schenone told us the story of Nike Presto during our interview in November 2007.

CHAPTER 9: WE ARE THEM AND THEY ARE US

Page 165—The Farbers' experiences were drawn from the OXO official history at its web site, an interview with Sam Farber from *@Issue,* the journal of the Corporate Design Foundation (volume 7, number 2), and from *Practically Edible,* an extensive food encyclopedia on the Internet.

Page 167—All of Pattie Moore's stories come from our April 8, 2008, interview.

Page 172—Mike Keefe's entire interview, including some of the amazing stuff we left out, took place on a rare Leap Day, February 29, 2008.

Page 178—*The Arizona Republic* covered the Australian study connecting friendship to life span in the article "Friendship, Not Family, Bonds May Increase Life Span," published June 28, 2006. Bio-medicine.org reprints the article.

Page 178—Lee Iacocca wrote about Ford's living-wage plan in *Time* magazine's 1998 "Time 100" issue, published December 7, 1998.

CHAPTER 10: THE GOLDEN RULE

Page 182—The *San Jose/Silicon Valley Business Journal* covered the fate of the CEO of Brocade on December 6, 2007, in the article "Former Brocade HR Chief Convicted in Options Case." The article discussed the conviction of another Brocade executive in addition to CEO Gregory Reyes.

Page 182—Many publications covered the options scandal well, but none with so much verve as *The Register,* whose March 16, 2007, article "Apple to Unbackdate (Some) Stock Options," by Chris Williams, does a concise but thorough job of covering everything that went down.

Page 184—We interviewed Cisco General Counsel and Senior Vice President Mark Chandler at his San Jose, California, office on April 7, 2008.

Page 186—Cisco's earnings come from the company's own annual report of August 7, 2007.

Page 187—As of 2008, Cisco ranked number 71 on the Fortune 500, behind only Intel (60) and HP (14) among Silicon Valley firms. The full list is online at *Fortune*'s web site.

Page 188—John H. Barrows organized the World's Parliament of Religion. His 1893 book, *World's Parliament of Religion,* from Parliament Publishing Company, details the complete proceedings of the event.

Page 189—Dr. Donald W. Pfaff's *The Neuroscience of Fair Play* contains his postulated four-step neurological process for the Golden Rule in pages 62 through 79. The book was published in 2007 by Dana Press.

Page 191—William Damon chronicled the youth who had no remorse for beating an elderly woman in his article "The Moral Development of Children," which was published in the August 1999 issue of *Scientific American.*

Page 192—Reuters reported on Northwest's pamphlet "Preparing for a Financial Setback" on August 15, 2006. Frank Langfitt of NPR's "Your Money" covered it in depth on August 23, 2006. The Northwest spokesman, Roman Blahoski, was quoted in the

Reuters article "Northwest Airlines to Workers: Look Through the Trash to Save Money."

Page 195—Google's controversial censorship of its Google.cn site was aptly dissected in the BBC News article "Google censors itself for China," published on Jan. 25, 2006.

Page 197—Rudy Giuliani's comments about waterboarding, and McCain's quotes in response, were reported by Michael Cooper and Marc Santora of *The New York Times* in the October 26, 2007, article "McCain Rebukes Giuliani on Waterboarding Remark."

Page 197—Mitt Romney's comments on waterboarding were drawn from the November 28, 2007, Republican primary debate shown on CNN and moderated by Anderson Cooper for the channel.

Page 197—John McCain wrote extensively about his imprisonment during the Vietnam War in the May 14, 1973, issue of *U.S. News and World Report.* That memoir, "John McCain, Prisoner of War: A First-Person Account," was made available online January 28, 2008.

CHAPTER 11: THE HIDDEN PAYOFF

Page 200—We interviewed Chip Conley on March 27, 2008.

Page 200—The lodging industry turnover rate was drawn from an article issued by Cornell University's Center for Hospitality Research on July 19, 2005. Professor Timothy R. Hinkin cites the figure as more than 65 percent per year.

Page 201—Chip Conley tells the story of the housekeeping experiment at Joie de Vivre at Amazon.com's home page for his wonderful book, *Peak: How Great Companies Get Their Mojo from Maslow,* published in late 2007 by Jossey-Bass Publishing.

Page 205—Gandhi's experiences and act of defiance at the Indian National Congress are discussed in *Gandhi's Pilgrimage of Faith: From Darkness to Light,* by Uma Majmudar and Rajmohan Gandhi, on page 123 of the 2005 edition published by State University of New York Press.

Index

A

abstractions
    making tangible
        Disney example, 36-38
        immediacy in, 38-39
    maps as, 19-23
actions, biological basis for,
    93-95
    Lawrence Taylor example,
        96-98
    limitations of, 98-99
Adstar, 30
affinity
    Bill Clinton presidential
        campaign example, 73-78
    biological reasons for, 71-73

loss of, 78-84
        *American automakers
        example,* 80-83
    Xbox example, 67-71
airline industry example,
    39-41
Allard, J., 70
American automakers
    example, 80-83
American Express, 29, 33
American Girl, 12-13, 99
AMF, 174
amygdala, 114
Animal Kingdom, 36-38
Apple, 16-17

automakers example, 80-83
Avedis Zildjian Company,
  50-58

B

Bachus, Kevin, 69
Back-to-School campaign
  example, 146-150
Ballmer, Steve, 30
Banks, Carl, 98
Bear Hug. *See* Operation Bear
  Hug (IBM)
Beck, Harry, 20-21
Beebe, Gina, 12-13, 99
Berkes, Otto, 69
biological basis
  for affinity, 71-73
  for emotional resonance
    from memories, 112-114
  for ethical behavior, 189-192
  for walking in others'
    shoes, 93-95
      Lawrence Taylor
      example, 96-98
      limitations of, 98-99
Blackley, Seamus, 67-71, 214
Bodegger, Sandy, 101
The Body Silent (Murphy), 92
Boeing, 5

Bowerman, Bill, 100, 157
brain, limbic system, 112-114
  emotional context
    provided by, 122-123
Brocade, 182
Bush, George H.W., 74, 76-79
Bush, George W., 78
business, lack of empathy in,
  115-116

C

call to service, 202-203, 213-215
  Clorox example, 209-213
  Gandhi example, 203-207
  Joie de Vivre example,
    200-202
  low-interest category
    products versus, 208-209
capitalism, London Farmers'
  Markets example, 61-63
caring. *See* empathy
Carnegie, Dale, 13, 104
Carville, Chester, 74
Carville, James, 73-78
Carville, Lucille, 74
Chambers, John, 183-187, 195
Chandler, Mark, 184, 187
Chrysler Corporation, 81, 83
Cisco Systems, 182-187, 195

Clinton, Bill, 73-78
Clorox, 152-154, 209-213
coffee industry example, 23-28
Colaiuta, Vinnie, 56
common man, connecting
    with, 203-207
companies
    creating empathy
        within, 124-125
    Open Empathy
    Organizations
        creating, 129-130
        employees as customers,
            133-135
        experiential nature of
            empathy, 137-138
        growth in, 138-139
        Nike example, 129
        open-windows analogy,
            130-133
        routine nature of empathy
            in, 135-137
    strategic planning, 127-128
company growth, empathy
    and, 6-8
Conley, Chip, 200-203

consumers
    producers as
        Harley-Davidson
            example, 172-178
        kitchen gadgets example,
            165-172
        value of, 178-179
    relationship with
    producers
        empathy in, 63-64
        Industrial Revolution,
            role of, 45-47
        London Farmers'
            Markets example, 58-63
        Play-Doh example, 42-45
        rift in, 46-50
        Zildjian Company
            example, 50-58
contextual knowledge. See
    intuition
COPCO, 166
corporations, lack of empathy
    in, 115-116
courage from face-to-face
    meetings with customers,
    108-110
curiosity, importance of, 104

customers
    connecting with. *See also*
        emotional resonance
        from memories
            Harley-Davidson
            example, 9-12
            Microsoft example, 14-18
            IBM example, 29-35
    disconnect from, 28-29
        Delta Airlines example,
        39-41
    employees as, 133-135
    face-to-face meetings with
        courage resulting from,
        108-110
        Mercedes-Benz example,
        105-108
    fulfilling expectations of,
    146-150
    similarity to
        Bill Clinton presidential
        campaign example,
        73-78
        biological reasons for,
        71-73
        loss of affinity, 78-84
        Xbox example, 67-71
cymbal industry example,
    50-58

D

Davidson, Willie G., 174-175
Davis, Muffy, 86-87, 91
Delta Airlines, 39-41
design challenges
    Play-Doh example, 42-45
    senior citizens, emulating
    experiences of, 3-5
Detroit, auto industry, 80-84
Disney, 36-38
disposable goods mentality,
    152-154
Dodge, 172-173
dogs, limbic system in, 113-114
DreamWorks Interactive, 68
drum industry example, 50-58
durable goods mentality,
    152-154

E

Eastman Kodak Company,
    154-156
economic history, Industrial
    Revolution in, 45-46
economy, labor statistics,
    119-120
Eisner, Michael, 36-38
elderly, emulating experiences
    of, 3-6
Ellison, Larry, 30

emotional context provided
by limbic system, 122-123
emotional resonance from
memories
  biological basis for, 112-114
  courage resulting from,
    108-110
  IBM example, 120-122
  Mercedes-Benz example,
    105-108
  Pixar example, 110-112
  Steelcase example, 116-119
empathy. *See also* customers,
connection with; ethical
behavior; producers, as
consumers; producers,
relationship with consumers
  affinity and
    *Bill Clinton presidential
    campaign example,
    73-78*
    *biological reasons for,
    71-73*
    loss of affinity, 78-84
    Xbox example, 67-71
  American Girl example,
    12-13
  company growth and, 6-8

creating within
  companies, 124-125
emotional resonance
  from memories
    *biological basis for,
    112-114*
    *courage resulting from,
    108-110*
    IBM example, 120-122
    *Mercedes-Benz example,
    105-108*
    Pixar example, 110-112
    Steelcase example, 116-119
  everyday practice of, 135-137
  experiential nature of,
    137-138
  Harley-Davidson example,
    9-12
  intuition and, 35-36
  lacking in corporations,
    115-116
  Microsoft example, 14-18
  Open Empathy
  Organizations
    creating, 129-130
    *employees as customers,
    133-135*

experiential nature of empathy, 137-138
growth in, 138-139
Nike example, 129
open-windows analogy, 130-133
routine nature of empathy in, 135-137
in producer/consumer relationship, 63-64
producer/consumer rift and, 49
as reaching outside yourself, 12-14
reframes and, 143-144, 164
role in meaningful work, 202-203, 213-215
  Clorox example, 209-213
  Gandhi example, 203-207
  Joie de Vivre example, 200-202
routine nature of, 135-137
senior citizens, emulating experiences of (example), 3-6
walking in others' shoes
  biological basis for, 93-95
  Lawrence Taylor example, 96-98
  limitations of mirror neurons, 98-99
  Nike example, 99-104
  wheelchair example, 85-92
employees, as customers, 133-135
environmental, office, 130-133
ethical behavior
  biological basis for, 189-192
  Cisco Systems example, 182-187
  levels of Golden Rule, 194-196
  Northwest Airlines example, 192-194
  reciprocal altruism, 187-189
  stock options example, 180-187
  water-boarding as torture example, 196-199
everyday practice of empathy, 135-137
experiential nature of empathy, 137-138

F

facilities management example, 116-119
Fadiga, Luciano, 94
Farber, Sam and Betsey, 165-169

Farberware, 166
farmers' markets example,
  58-63
Fogassi, Leonardo, 94
Folgers, 24, 26
Ford, Henry, 80, 178-179
Ford Motor Company, 81-83
French Laundry
  (restaurant), 110-111
friendship, value of, 178

G

Gadd, Steve, 50
Gallese, Vittorio, 94
Gandhi, Mohandas, 203-207
Gates, Bill, 69
Geffen, David, 68
General Motors, 181, 183
Gerstner, Lou, 29-35, 120-122
gift-giving analogy, 107-108
Giuliani, Rudy, 196-197
Gokhale, Gopal Krishna,
  205-206
Golden Rule. See also ethical
  behavior
    levels of, 194-196
    religious/cultural nature
      of, 187-189
Google, 194-195
Gore, Al, 78

growth
  empathy and, 6-8
  in Open Empathy
    Organizations, 138-139
gut sense
  Disney example, 36-38
  importance of, 35-36
  role in empathy, 6

H

Halo (game), 16
Harley-Davidson, 9-12, 132,
  171-178
Hase, Ted, 69
Hatfield, Tinker, 101
Hatfield, Tobie, 161
Hills Bros., 24, 26
hippocampus, 114
Hoffer, Kevin, 161
Honda, 82
hotel housekeeping example,
  200-202
How to Win Friends and
  Influence People (Carnegie),
  13, 104
human connections
  biological basis for, 112-114
  courage resulting from,
    108-110

IBM example, 120-122
Mercedes-Benz example,
  105-108
Pixar example, 110-112
Steelcase example, 116-119

I

IBM, 29-35, 120-122, 132
immediacy needed in maps,
  36-39
    Delta Airlines example,
      39-41
    Disney example, 36-38
Industrial Revolution,
  45-50, 208
inference of needs, 150-154
information simplification
    coffee industry example,
      23-28
    dangers in, 19-23
    lack of context with, 28-29
Intel Corporation, 135
International Harvester,
  SRC (Springfield
  ReManufacturing Center),
  125-128
intuition
    Disney example, 36-38
    importance of, 35-36
    role in empathy, 6

isolationism
    avoiding, 179
    dangers of, 6

J

Jell-O, 84
Jenkins, Adrianna, 72
Jimbo, Akira, 56
job growth statistics, 119-120
Joie de Vivre, 200-202
Jones, Papa Jo, 54

K

K2 (sports equipment
  company), 47-48
Katzenberg, Jeffrey, 68
Keefe, Mike, 172-178, 214
Keller, Thomas, 110
Kiniry, Ed, 47-48
kitchen gadgets example,
  165-172
Knight, Phil, 100, 157
Kodak, 154-156
Korzybski, Alfred, 21
Krauss, Robert, 92
Krupa, Gene, 50, 54

L

labor statistics, 119-120
laid-off employees example,
  192-194

learning by observation, 95

Lee, Lara, 11, 171

Lewis, Brad, 110-112

Lexmark, 30

limbic system, 112-114
   emotional context
      provided by, 122-123

Loewy, Raymond, 170

London Farmers' Markets,
   58-63

London Underground, 19-22

low-interest category
   products, 208-209

M

maps. *See also* simplification
   of information
   as abstractions, 19-23
   immediacy needed in,
      36-39
      Delta Airlines example,
         39-41
      Disney example, 36-38

market forces, London
   Farmers' Markets example,
   61-63

The Matrix (film), 144

Maxwell House, 23-28

McCain, John, 197-198

McCartney, Paul, 113

McKinsey and Company, 29

meaningful work, 202-203,
   213-215
   Clorox example, 209-213
   Gandhi example, 203-207
   Joie de Vivre example,
      200-202
   low-interest category
      products versus, 208-209

memories, emotional
   resonance from
   biological basis for, 112-114
   courage resulting from,
      108-110
   IBM example, 120-122
   Mercedes-Benz example,
      105-108
   Pixar example, 110-112
   Steelcase example, 116-119

Mercedes-Benz, 105-109

Merck & Co., Inc., 5

Mervar, Bob, 162

Microsoft Corporation, 14-18,
   67-71, 79

Mintzberg, Henry, 128

mirror neurons, 93-95
   Lawrence Taylor example,
      96-98
   limitations of, 98-99

Moccasins project, 85

Moore, Pattie, 3-6, 166-170
moral behavior
    biological basis for, 189-192
    Cisco Systems example,
        182-187
    levels of Golden Rule,
        194-196
    Northwest Airlines
        example, 192-194
    reciprocal altruism, 187-189
    stock options example,
        180-187
    water-boarding as torture
        example, 196-199
motor neurons, 93-95
multiple reframes, 157
    Nike example, 157-163
multiple types of people,
    empathy for, 13
Murad IV, Sultan of the
    Ottoman Empire, 51
Murphy, Robert, 92

N
Needfinding class, 42, 85,
    151-152
needs, inferring, 150-154
neocortex, 112
Netflix, 134
Nike, 80, 99-104, 129-130, 132,
    138, 157-163

Nintendo, 15-16, 70, 79
Northwest Airlines, 192-194

O
observation, learning by, 95
office environment, 130-133
Ogilvy & Mather, 31
Oldham, Todd, 149
Olds, Ransom E., 80
open-book management,
    125-129
open-windows analogy,
    130-133
Open Empathy Organizations
    creating, 129-130
    employees as customers,
        133-135
    experiential nature of
        empathy, 137-138
    growth in, 137-138
    Nike example, 129
    open-windows analogy,
        130-133
    routine nature of empathy
        in, 135-137
Operation Bear Hug (IBM),
    120-122
organizations
    creating empathy
        within, 124-125

Open Empathy
Organizations
creating, 129-130
employees as customers,
133-135
experiential nature of
empathy, 137-138
growth in, 138
Nike example, 129
open-windows analogy,
130-133
routine nature of empathy
in, 135-137
strategic planning, 127-128
OXO, 169-170

P

Parker, Mark, 101, 162
Parliament of World
Religions, 188
Patagonia, 195-196
pattern identification, 21
Peak (Conley), 200
Perot, Ross, 77
Pfaff, Donald, 189-190
Pixar, 110-112
Planck, Nina, 58-63, 214
Play-Doh example (design
challenges), 42-45
premotor cortex, 93

presidential campaign (1992)
example, 73-78
producers
as consumers
Harley-Davidson
example, 172-178
kitchen gadgets example,
165-172
value of, 178-179
relationship with
consumers
empathy in, 63-64
Industrial Revolution,
role of, 45-50
London Farmers'
Markets example, 58-63
Play-Doh example, 42-45
rift in, 46-50
Zildjian Company
example, 50-58

Q–R

Ratatouille (film), 110-112
Raymond Loewy (industrial
design firm), 3
reciprocal altruism, 187-189
reframes, 143-146
empathy and, 144-145, 164
multiple reframes, 157
Nike example, 157-163

transformative power of,
156-157
types of, 145-146
   Clorox example, 150-154
   fulfilling customer
      expectations, 146-150
   inference of needs, 150-154
   innovative solutions,
      154-156
   Kodak example, 154-156
   Target example, 146-150
regulation, market forces
   versus, 61
religion, Golden Rule and,
   187-189
reptilian brain, 112-113
Republican presidential
   candidates, views on
   water-boarding as torture,
   196-199
Reyes, Greg, 182
Rheinfrank, John, 154-156
Rich, Buddy, 50
The Rise and Fall of Strategic
   Planning (Mintzberg), 128
Rizzolatti, Giacomo, 94
RJR Nabisco, 29
Rohde, Joe, 36-38
Romney, Mitt, 197

S

Salvador, Tony, 135
Schenone, Dave, 99-104,
   157-163, 214
Schultz, Howard, 27
senior citizens, emulating
   experiences of, 3-5
Sheffield Silver, 166
Sick Building Syndrome, 131
similarity to customers
   Bill Clinton presidential
      campaign example, 73-78
   biological reasons for, 71-73
   loss of affinity, 78-84
      American automakers
         example, 80-83
   Xbox example, 67-71
simplification of information
   coffee industry example,
      23-28
   dangers in, 19-23
   lack of context with, 28-29
Smart Design, 166-168
Smith & Hawken, 137
solutions, as reframes, 154-156
Sony Corporation, 15-16,
   68-71
Spalding, 136-137
Spielberg, Steven, 68

sports fashion example, 157-163

SRC (Springfield ReManufacturing Center), 125-128

Stack, Jack, 125-127

Starbucks, 27, 104

Starr, Ringo, 50

Steelcase Corporation, 116-119

stock options example, 180-187

strategic planning, 127-128

street smarts. *See* intuition

Strungk, Nicolaus, 52

success, loss of affinity from, 78-80

T

Tandem Computers, 100

tangibility of abstractions
  Disney example, 36-38
  immediacy in, 38-39

Target, 133-134, 146-150

Taylor, Lawrence, 96-98

Theismann, Joe, 97-98

torture example, 196-199

Toyota, 5, 82

Tubbs Snowshoe Company, 47-48

U–V

University of Oregon, 100

Viemeister, Tucker, 168

W

walking in others' shoes
  biological basis for, 93-95
  Lawrence Taylor example, 96-98
  limitations of mirror neurons, 98-99
  Nike example, 99-104
  wheelchair example, 86-92

water-boarding as torture example, 196-199

Webb, Chick, 54

We're Right, They're Wrong (Carville), 75

wheelchair example, 86-92

Wii (Nintendo), 79

work, meaning in, 202-203, 213-215
  Clorox example, 209-213
  Gandhi example, 203-207
  Joie de Vivre example, 200-202
  low-interest category products versus, 207-209

worldview, reframing, 143-146
empathy and, 143-144, 164
multiple reframes, 157
Nike example, 157-163
transformative power of,
156-157
types of reframes, 145-146
Clorox example, 150-154
fulfilling customer
expectations, 146-150
inference of needs, 150-154
innovative solutions,
154-156
Kodak example, 154-156
Target example, 146-150

X–Z
Xbox, 14, 16, 17, 67-71, 79

Zildjian, Aram, 52-53
Zildjian, Armand, 55-56
Zildjian, Avedis, 50-51
Zildjian, Avedis III, 52-55
Zildjian, Kerope, 52
Zildjian Company, 50-58
Zune, 17

About the Authors

Dev Patnaik is a founder and principal of Jump Associates, an innovation strategy firm. He has been an advisor to some of the world's most admired companies, including GE, Target, Nike, and Harley-Davidson. Dev is an adjunct faculty member at Stanford University, where he teaches Needfinding to design and business school students. He lives in the San Francisco Bay Area.

Peter Mortensen is the communications lead at Jump Associates and a blog contributor for *Wired*.

FINANCIAL TIMES

In an increasingly competitive world, it is quality
of thinking that gives an edge—an idea that opens new
doors, a technique that solves a problem, or an insight
that simply helps make sense of it all.

We work with leading authors in the various arenas
of business and finance to bring cutting-edge thinking
and best-learning practices to a global market.

It is our goal to create world-class print publications
and electronic products that give readers
knowledge and understanding that can then be
applied, whether studying or at work.

To find out more about our business
products, you can visit us at www.ftpress.com.